KANT

Moral Legislation and Two Senses of 'Will'

Gary M. Hochberg
Bucknell University

UNIVERSITY
PRESS OF
AMERICA

Copyright © 1982 by

University Press of America, Inc.

P.O. Box 19101, Washington, D.C. 20036

Library of Congress Catalog Card Number: 81-40396

For June, Mark, and Amy,

without whom this would not have been worthwhile

ACKNOWLEDGEMENTS

No work of scholarship can be completed without assistance in various forms. I take pleasure in recognizing a number of individuals and organizations without whose cooperation and help this book could not have been published.

Permission to quote from other works has been granted by both individuals and publishing companies. I am grateful to James W. Ellington for permission to quote from his translation of Kant's Metaphysical Principles of Virtue; to Richard McKeon for his Introduction to Aristotle; to Bobbs-Merrill Educational Publishing for permission to quote from the following: L. W. Beck, Studies in the Philosophy of Kant (Essay and Monograph Series of the Liberal Arts Press, Copyright 1965), David Hume, An Inquiry Concerning the Principles of Morals (Liberal Arts Press, Copyright, 1957), Immanuel Kant, Critique of Practical Reason (Bobbs-Merrill Company, Inc., Copyright 1956), Kant, Foundations of the Metaphysics of Morals, (Liberal Arts Press, Copyright, 1959), Kant, The Metaphysical Elements of Justice (Liberal Arts Press, Copyright, 1965), J. S. Mill, Utilitarianism (Liberal Arts Press, Copyright, 1957); finally, to Harper Torch Books for permission to quote from R. P. Wolff's The Autonomy of Reason.

Two other individuals deserve special thanks for their contributions to this work, one for extremely tangible contributions, the other for invaluable intangible aid. Judy Gilbert did what I believe to be the best typing job in the history of modern publishing, enabling me to worry about other matters while the manuscript was being prepared. In directing my dissertation just over a decade ago, John Ladd kindled an interest in Kant's moral theory which burns to this day, and for this I am in his debt. He will almost certainly not agree with all that I have to say, but I hope he will see the mark of his influence.

TABLE OF CONTENTS

Kant: Moral Legislation and Two Senses of 'Will'

Introduction.

     Kant's moral philosophy has two distinct, though closely related aspects or facets, one descriptive, the other normative or prescriptive. What I term the 'descriptive' side of Kant's theory deals with those metaphysical assumptions Kant thinks it is necessary to make to account for our sense of obligation to the categorical imperative or moral law. Kant's theory of freedom, and the doctrines of the <u>Critique of Pure Reason</u>[1] regarding the distinction between appearances and things-in-themselves are crucial to this feature of Kant's moral theory. The 'normative' dimension of Kant's theory has the concept of universal self-legislation as its primary focus.

     In his famous <u>Grundlegung</u>, Kant runs the two aspects of his theory together somewhat, in asking how a categorical imperative is possible.[2] Central to both dimensions of the theory is the concept of the rational will, and the distinction drawn by Kant between two different senses of 'will': <u>Wille</u>, or the legislative faculty; <u>Willkür</u>, or the faculty of choice. Kant does not make an explicit distinction between these two senses of 'will' in the <u>Grundlegung</u>, and this may account for the fact that the two facets of his moral theory seem to be somewhat conflated at points in this work. An understanding of the nature of this distinction is essential to comprehending Kant's various claims about the 'causality' of the will, and about the binding force of the categorical imperative. I treat the distinction between the two senses of 'will', and the concept of moral legislation which is possible because of the distinction as the central notions in Kant's moral theory. Although the distinction has been noted by many commentators, I do not think that its significance has been fully appreciated.

The work consists of the following four chapters:

Chapter I. Two Senses of 'Will': A Preliminary Sketch. In this first chapter, I present a preliminary analysis of the Wille/Willkür distinction, and of the relation between them; a sketch of Kant's view that morality requires 'intrinsically practical reason', and thus more than Hume's position allows; a treatment of the concept of a 'holy will'; the concept of 'choice', with an emphasis on relations between Kant and Aristotle; Kant's concept of a 'maxim' and the problems of 'alternative act-descriptions' and moral epistemology. Readers who are hoping to find an answer 'once and for all' to the old query as to how it is that the categorical imperative determines how one ought to act in each and every instance will be disappointed in my treatment of these last issues, because, for reasons I discuss in Chapter IV, I do not think that this is what Kant wanted the categorical imperative to do, nor do I think that it is reasonable to require that it do so, quite apart from what Kant may have had in mind.

Chapter II. Kant's Theories of the 'Causality' of the Will: this chapter, essential to understanding what I have termed the 'descriptive' or 'metaphysical' side of Kant's moral theory, contains an analysis of Aristotle's doctrine of 'four causes' as a key to understanding Kant; the faculty of choice (Willkür) as spontaneous efficient cause; analysis of the Third Antinomy and the Second Analogy sections of the first Critique; the 'causality' of the legislative faculty (Wille) as formal and final cause; the 'causality' of the joint or combined faculty of the will. It will be immediately apparent that many of the views for which I argue in this chapter are divergent from standard interpretations of Kant, and I take issue with the work of several commentators, including Beck, Silber, and Wolff.

Chapter III. Legislation and the Distinction
Between Wille and Willkür: this chapter deals with
what I have termed the 'normative' dimension of
Kant's argument, and includes an analysis of the
concept of autonomy; legislation and the faculty
of choice; the possibility of hypothetical imperatives; the theory of moral legislation; internal
and external legislation; Kant's critique of utilitarian conceptions of internal and external sanctions, including references to Bentham, Hume, and
J. S. Mill; legislation and obligation; Kant and
the tradition of social contract theory, including
Hobbes, Rousseau, and John Rawls. I argue that
Kant's theory of obligation is best understood in
terms of its relations to contract theory, with
Rawls' contractarianism being the closest to
Kant's. I do not spend time on recent critiques
of Rawls' theory, such as Brian Barry's The Liberal
Theory of Justice,[3] R. P. Wolff's Understanding
Rawls,[4] and Norman Daniels' collection of essays,
Reading Rawls.[5] These are all serious works, and
deserve serious, and separate, treatment. My concern here has been to show how I think Kant's view
is best understood, and not to defend the theory
(that of Rawls) in terms of which we can make sense
of Kant. I do think that most of the criticisms
of Rawls' Kantianism miss the mark somewhat, but
showing this would involve too much of a digression
from my main purposes.

Chapter IV. Concluding Remarks and Lingering
Difficulties: in this final chapter, I try to
deal with objections to the foregoing chapters,
and with some of the positions taken in the secondary literature. The chapter contains: problems
with the concept of 'autonomy'; Jeffrie Murphy's
account of the origins of 'dignity'; spontaneity
vs. autonomy; Kant's answer to the question 'Why
should I be moral?'; a critique of Wolff's The
Autonomy of Reason[6]; a defense of the contract
model of Kant's theory of obligation. In this
chapter, I recur to an issue raised in Chapter I,
that of whether the categorical imperative can be
employed to determine what specific action one
ought to perform in each and every instance. I

3

argue that it cannot, that Kant did not intend
that it should, and also that it is quite un-
reasonable that it should be able to determine
our specific obligations in each and every case.
On this question, I find myself quite at odds
with Professor Wolff's views in The Autonomy of
Reason.

Despite the extent to which some of my
analyses of Kant diverge from positions taken in
the secondary literature, I do think that there
are ample grounds for the lines of interpretation
I take, and that many of the difficulties that
remain in some of the other commentaries can be
removed by adopting my views. The reader will
have to make an independent judgment as to the
value of my arguments. Given the subject of this
work, this seems most fitting.

NOTES - Introduction

[1]Kant, <u>Critique of Pure Reason</u> (Kemp-Smith translation). Henceforth, this work will be referred to as the first <u>Critique</u> in the text, and as <u>Critique I</u> in notes. All pagination is from the Akademie edition.

[2]Kant, <u>Foundations of the Metaphysics of Morals</u> (Beck translation). Henceforth, this work will be referred to as the <u>Grundlegung</u> in the text, and as <u>FMM</u> in notes. All pagination is from the Akademie edition.

[3]Brian Barry, <u>The Liberal Theory of Justice</u> (Oxford: 1973).

[4]Robert Paul Wolff, <u>Understanding Rawls</u> (Princeton: 1976).

[5]<u>Reading Rawls</u>, edited by Norman Daniels (Basic Books: 1976).

[6]Robert Paul Wolff, <u>The Autonomy of Reason</u> (Harper Torchbooks: 1973).

Chapter I. Two Senses of 'Will': A Preliminary
Sketch.

There are many issues in Kant's moral philosophy that turn on the distinction between Wille
and Willkür. His theory of obligation really
makes little sense without the distinction; nor
does the concept of autonomous legislation, which
is so crucial for Kant's theory of obligation;
further, the notion of the 'causality' of the will
is intelligible, I think, only in terms of the distinction between two senses of 'will'. These and
other matters can be understood best (and perhaps
only) in light of the distinction. Thus it is
imperative that one get clear about the nature of
the Wille/Willkür distinction at the outset of a
study of Kant's moral theory. Here, I shall give
only a preliminary sketch of the distinction. As
other material is introduced later, it will be
possible to amplify certain points made here, but
a rough sketch of the distinction is required to
make any progress at all. Thus, a full discussion
of many of the issues raised here will be post-
poned until later chapters.

A. Wille and Willkür.

Kant distinguishes between Wille and Willkür,
two German terms which may be translated as 'will',
but which have very different meanings. The
difference in meaning is essential to Kant's moral
theory. It is a distinction which is not explicitly drawn in the Grundlegung, but which does
appear in such later writings as the Metaphysics
of Morals and Religion Within the Limits of Reason
Alone. It is also worth noting that Kant refers to
the will as Willkür in the Critique of Pure Reason.[1]
This may seem a bit strange, and perhaps not in
keeping with Kant's discussion of the will as a
'causality' in the Grundlegung.[2] I shall discuss
this matter in some detail at the proper time.

The term Wille, frequently translated as 'Will'

(upper-case 'W') in translations of Kant's later
ethical writings, is used to refer to the legislative aspect of the will. Of the <u>Wille</u>, Kant
writes,

> Laws proceed from the Will . . .
> The Will, which relates to nothing
> but the law, cannot be called either
> free or unfree, for it relates,
> not to actions, but immediately to
> legislation for the maxims of
> action . . . Consequently, it is
> absolutely necessary and is it-
> self incapable of constraint.[3]

I shall argue later that, while it is correct for
Kant to say that the Will is neither free nor unfree in one sense, it would not be reasonable to
attribute all that he says about 'freedom' to 'will'
in the sense of the faculty of choice. We shall
see more of this later.

The term <u>Willkür</u>, commonly translated as 'will'
(lower-case 'w') in translations of Kant's later
writings, is used to refer to the faculty of choice
within the will. A rough English equivalent of
the meaning of <u>Willkür</u> is either 'arbitrariness'
or 'spontaneity'. Of course, Kant does not wish
for moral choices to be thought of as <u>arbitrary</u>,
but there is a sense in which this is the appropriate term to use in this context. Again, we shall
see more of this later. For the present moment,
I am concerned only to draw the distinction between the two senses of 'will' in a preliminary
way. Of the <u>Willkür</u>, Kant writes,

> The faculty of desiring in accord-
> ance with concepts is called the
> faculty of doing or forbearing as
> one likes . . . insofar as the
> ground determining it to action
> is found in the faculty of desire
> itself and not in the object. In-
> sofar as it is combined with the

8

consciousness of the capacity
of its action to produce its
object, it is called will or
choice [Willkür];[4]

Here, when Kant says that the ground determining
the faculty of desire to action must be found in
the faculty of desire itself, rather than in the
object, we must take care not to take this as
meaning that all choices are autonomous, where
this refers to the capacity of the will to be a
'law to itself'.[5] I think it is clear that Kant
would say that we can and do make heteronomous
choices. Indeed, his analysis of freedom and the
possibility of 'radical evil' in Religion Within
the Limits of Reason Alone make this quite clear.
This, again, is a topic to be taken up in more
detail later on.

     How, then, should we characterize the dis-
tinction between Wille and Willkür? One might
be tempted to interpret the distinction between
the two senses of 'will' as that between the
passive and active aspects of one faculty. As
we shall see, however, this would be misleading
in the case of Kant's theory. Human action is,
for Kant, the result of choice, and choice is the
function of the Willkür.[6] Kant sometimes defines
the Will as practical reason itself.[7] Since the
Wille, as practical reason is not the faculty
of choice and choice is, as I have said, a condition of the possibility of human action, we
might say that Wille is not active. However,
Wille is taken, by Kant, to be a determining
ground of the faculty of choice. Thus, it would
be misleading to say merely that the faculty of
choice is active, while the Wille is passive.
Saying that the Wille is passive also gives the
impression that something is done to it, and, as
we shall see, this is not the case. It is more
accurate to say that the Wille does not choose,
while choosing is the very essence of the Willkür.
As I shall show later on, it is helpful to think
of Kant's concept of the Wille as being analogous
to Aristotle's concept of a prime, or unmoved mover.

9

What is the function of the Will, considered as <u>Wille</u>, or practical reason? Its function is said by Kant to be to 'determine' the <u>Willkür</u>, or the faculty of choice, to act in accordance with the moral law. It is well to note that this function is expressed in the following passage from Kant's <u>Grundlegung</u>:

> . . . reason is given to us as a practical faculty, i.e., one which is meant to have an influence on the will. As nature has elsewhere distributed capacities suitable to the functions they are to perform, reason's proper function must be to produce a will good in itself and not only good merely as a means, for to the former reason is absolutely essential.[8]

Kant is arguing here that reason's proper function in relation to conduct cannot be to lead us to happiness. Kant says this because, first, he thinks that, ". . . no organ will be found for any purpose which is not the fittest and best adapted to that purpose."[9], and, second, that,

> . . . if its preservation, its welfare - in a word, its happiness - were the real end of nature in a being having reason and will, then nature would have hit upon a very poor arrangement in appointing the reason of the creature to be the executor of this purpose. For all the actions which the creature has to perform with this intention, and the entire rule of its conduct, would be dictated much more exactly by instinct, and that end would be far more certainly attained by instinct than it ever could be by reason.[10]

10

We may ask how reasonable it is for Kant to assume
that no organ is ever found for a purpose to which
it is not the best suited. Whether this is reasonable depends on what is meant. One could take
Kant as meaning that any organ whatever is always
the best suited to its purpose - which would lead
us to the absurd consequence that both the human
eye and the fish's eye are the best suited to seeing, or that the human leg and the frog's leg are
both the best suited to jumping. But this is
silly, and I assume that it is not what Kant intended. What he probably does mean is that, within a given creature, no organ is found for a purpose for which some other organ of the same
creature is better suited. This seems to me very
likely to be true and, at the least, it is a long
way from being absurd, particularly when we recall
that Kant makes this claim about what he calls
'well-organized' beings, those suited for life.

If we grant Kant's point about the 'proper
function' of reason, we still have to understand
wherein that very important function consists.
In this connection, a word concerning the concept of 'determination' is in order here. The
German verb which has been translated as 'to determine' is *bestimmen*. The term has several
other acceptable translations in addition to
'determine', including: 'regulate', 'specify',
and 'influence'. I believe that the term 'determine', as it is ordinarily used in English, is
too strong to express what Kant sees as the actual
relationship between <u>Wille</u> and <u>Willkür</u>. 'Determine' generally suggests a relationship which
cannot be other than it is. That is, if I claim
to have been 'determined' to a life of crime, I
am presumably asserting that I could not choose
otherwise. The relation between <u>Wille</u> and <u>Willkür</u>
is, as we shall see, weaker than <u>this</u>. Indeed,
it must be weaker if Kant's concept of obligation
is to make any sense at all. Kant does on
occasion use the weaker term 'influence' (*Einfluss*,
in German) to describe the relation between the
two senses of 'will'. For example, Kant writes,

11

". . . reason is given to us as a practical faculty, i.e., one which is meant to have an influence on the will."[11]

Indeed, when Kant speaks of reason (Wille)
determining the will (Willkür), he does so in an
hypothetical mode, saying, "If reason infallibly
determines the will, the actions which such a
being recognizes as objectively necessary are also
subjectively necessary."[12] Kant makes it clear
that such infallible determination is not the
nature of the relationship that obtains between
the Wille and the human faculty of choice. I
think that we might term the relation between
Wille and the human faculty of choice to be one
of normative determination, but I shall say more
about this later.

We should guard against a possible confusion here. Although it is the case that the
relation between Wille and the human Willkür is
weaker than what we ordinarily understand by
the term 'determination', this does not mean that
the relation is a contingent one. Rather, though
it may be a contingent matter whether the faculty
of choice follows the dictates of the legislative
faculty of the will, it is not a contingent
matter that the legislative faculty makes its
demands. The demands of the legislative faculty
are objectively necessary, though they may be
subjectively contingent.[13] We shall see more
about this when we discuss what is meant in calling reason 'intrinsically practical'.

As a prelude to what is to come later, it is
also worth noting that, when Kant refers to reason
as a ". . . practical faculty, i.e., one which is
meant to have an influence on the will."[14], he is
using 'will' in the sense of Willkür. Kant does
not use the term Willkür in the original German
text at this stage, but, as I have said, the distinction between the two senses of 'will' is one
that Kant does not make explicitly in the
Grundlegung at all. For reasons that will become

12

clear later, it makes sense to interpret Kant as referring to 'will' in the sense of Willkür in the passage just mentioned. It is my view that Kant's position in the Grundlegung can be understood only in terms of an implicit distinction between the two senses of 'will'. It is both illuminating and entertaining to go through the Grundlegung to decide which sense of 'will' Kant is intending each time the term appears. Unfortunately, however, this task is also too time-consuming for us to engage in it here.

B. 'Intrinsically Practical' Reason.

As we have seen, Kant refers to the will, apparently in the sense of Wille, as 'practical reason itself'. Moreover, we have asserted that Kant's moral philosophy requires a reason which is 'intrinsically practical'. Let us now examine this assertion in more detail. What is meant in saying that reason can be 'intrinsically practical', and why does Kant's moral theory require such? I shall say, with Lewis White Beck, that reason is 'intrinsically practical' if, "It establishes the goals of action through the formulation of an intrinsically practical and unconditional law."[15] This passage is difficult to interpret. Notice that it cannot, strictly speaking, be a definition of 'intrinsically practical reason', because the phrase 'intrinsically practical' occurs in both the definiens and the definiendum. Something is said to be 'practical' when it has relevance for action. Indeed, according to Beck, reason establishes the goals of action.

In order to distinguish Kant's view from that of, say, David Hume, however, it is necessary to state precisely what is meant in calling reason 'relevant' to action. Reason is 'relevant' for action on Hume's view also, but only as a tool for calculating how a given interest might best be served. This is not enough for Kant.

Let us be clear that Hume's views regarding

13

the relation of reason to conduct are those I have
ascribed to him. The following passages are
illustrative of the sort of position Hume adopts:

> I shall endeavour to prove first,
> that reason alone can never be a
> motive to any action of the will;
> and, secondly, that it can never
> oppose passion in the direction
> of the will.[16]

And, further,

> Abstract or demonstrative reasoning
> . . . never influences any of our
> actions . . . Since reason alone can
> never produce any action, or give
> rise to volition, I infer that the
> same faculty is as incapable of
> preventing volition, or of disputing
> with any passion or emotion.[17]

From these passages it is obvious that, for Hume,
reason can never of itself be a motive for action.
This is not to say, of course, that reason does
not serve to calculate the most efficient course
to take in the pursuit of some end dictated by
desire.

It is clear from the above that, if Kant's
view is to be significantly different from that of
Hume, it must be the case that there is something
unique about the sense in which, for Kant, reason
is 'practical'. Kant's view seems to include that
of Hume, in that reason can indeed be employed to
calculate the best way to serve a given interest.
But Kant goes further than Hume, proposing that
reason can, of itself, establish the goals of
action without being dependent upon a reference
to a desire to be fulfilled through the action.
For reason to be 'intrinsically practical' means
that it can establish the goals of action without
having to appeal to anything to be gained in performing a given action. That is, reason must be

14

able to establish the goals of action without having to appeal to any merely subjective purpose to be served in performing the action. I understand this last point to mean that reason establishes formal limits to which actions must conform, or ought to conform. I say 'merely subjective purpose' here, because I wish to emphasize the fact that Kant's quarrel is not so much with subjective purposes (desires) per se, as it is with the attempt, much promoted by moralists of the utilitarian stripe, to ground morality on 'merely subjective purposes'.

In fairness to Hume, it should be noted that his view is not as different from Kant's own position as the above-cited passages from the *Treatise* may suggest. It is clear that Hume is speaking of what Kant calls speculative or theoretical reason when he denies the possibility of reason's directly influencing conduct. Kant would certainly agree with Hume concerning the inability of speculative reason to influence conduct directly. For example, Kant writes, "*Knowledge*, which as such is speculative, can have no other object than that supplied by experience;"[18] Or, regarding the distinction between the speculative and practical employments of human reason, ". . . when we consider these actions in their relation to reason - I do not mean speculative reason, by which we endeavour *to explain* their coming into being, but reason insofar as it is itself the cause *producing* them -"[19] Or, again, ". . . theoretical knowledge may be defined as knowledge of what *is*, practical knowledge as the representation of what *ought to be*."[20] Thus, Kant's disagreement with Hume is not over the nature and capacities of speculative reason in relation to conduct but, rather, over the question whether reason may not also have a uniquely practical employment. Kant's conclusion, of course, is that there must be such a practical employment of reason, if our common-sense conceptions of the categorical requirements of morality are to be vindicated. As Kant says,

> . . . reason is given to us as a
> practical faculty, i.e., one which
> is meant to have an influence on
> the will . . . reason's proper func-
> tion must be to produce a will good
> in itself and not only good merely
> as a means, for to the former reason
> is absolutely essential.[21]

Let us pause briefly to relate what we have
learned from this discussion of the notion of 'intrinsically practical reason' to the preceding
analysis of Kant's concept of 'determination'.
Given what was said about 'determination', it is
clear that, in thinking of reason as 'intrinsically practical', Kant cannot mean that reason
'always has its way' without fail. For, if reason
necessarily 'had its way', there would be no need
for constraint, nor for any theory of moral obligation, either. What Kant evidently means in
terming reason 'intrinsically practical' is that
reason always, necessarily, exerts pressure on
the faculty of choice, in the attempt to have its
choices comply. We shall see more about the notion
of a practical reason that 'always has its way'
when we discuss the concept of a 'holy will' later.
We should note, too, that all of what has been
said here pertains to practical reason in its relation to the human will, since it is precisely
the human faculty of choice which is only incompletely determined by practical reason.

To return to the central theme of this chapter, let us consider the nature of the relation
between the two senses of 'will'. As has been
noted, the relation between Wille and Willkür is
one of 'determination'. This, as we have seen,
may be taken to mean 'rendering it necessary that
such-and-such occur'. But, while Kant does wish
to say that what is moral is also 'necessary', it
is clear that this is a different sense of 'necessity' from that of the relation of cause and effect
in the phenomenal world, or, at least, it is a
different application of necessity.[22] To say that
one event determines another in the phenomenal

world is to say that, given the first event, the
second must occur. This is not the nature of the
determination of Willkür by Wille. To say that
the Wille expresses the moral law does not guarantee that the faculty of choice will choose according to the demands of the moral law, or out of
respect for the moral law.

But, as we have said, there is yet a further
sense of the concept of 'determination' which is
appropriate to the relation between the two senses
of 'will'. And, while Kant clearly does not think
that the legislative faculty determines the faculty of choice in precisely the same way as physical
events are determined, there does seem to be what
we might call a 'normative analogue' to the determination of physical events. That is, just
as physical laws determine, in a formal way, what
can happen, so practical (normative) laws determine
in a formal way what ought to happen. There are
several issues that would need to be discussed here,
in order to make the present matters clear: Kant's
analysis of the Third Antinomy; the concept of the
'causality' of the will. These discussions will
be necessary if we are to make sense of the way in
which 'determination' expresses the relation between the two senses of 'will'. I will postpone
these considerations until a later chapter, however,
at which time I will examine them in some detail.

Kant employs the notion of 'determination',
I think, in order to establish a certain symmetry
between moral and natural law. He writes "[By
analogy], then, the universal imperative of duty
can be expressed as follows: Act as though the
maxim of your action were by your will to become
a universal law of nature."[23] I think this passage makes clear the sense of symmetry Kant wishes
to develop between the phenomenal and moral realms.
There are different senses of necessity involved
here, as is evidenced by the different Latin expressions Kant takes as keys. He writes, "An
obligation implies not that an action is necessary merely, but that it is made necessary; it is
not a question of *necessitas*, but of *necessitatio*."[24]

17

Once again, of course, it is important to note that the phrase 'made necessary' as it is employed here does not mean the same thing that it does in speaking of physical necessitation. Kant is referring to the notion of an action's being made necessary from a normative point of view.

There is another observation that should be raised here, in order to guard against confusion. As we shall see later, there are three different ways of speaking of the 'causality' of the will, or the 'making necessary' of actions by the will. One sense centers on the Wille, a second on Willkür, while the third focuses on the entire rational faculty of the will. Aristotle's analysis of four senses of 'cause' is relevant to understanding Kant's position on these points. We shall see much more about this later.

In the passage just cited, I think it makes most sense to interpret Kant as meaning that Wille's legislation makes an action necessary for Willkür. The alternative here is to suppose that the faculty of choice has made some action necessary and, while Kant does indeed want to account for the possibility of this, it would not make sense to speak of obligation in this vein: obligation is a normative concept, referring to what actions we ought to set ourselves to do; choice, in and of itself, refers to what we actually do set ourselves to do. As we shall see later, in our analysis of Kant's resolution of the Third Antinomy, and in a discussion of the 'causality' of the will, the possibility of the Willkur's making actions necessary is a necessary condition of Wille's being able to make actions morally necessary, i.e., obligatory.

Since the Wille necessarily expresses the moral law, the responsibility for the realization of moral action must lie with the faculty of choice. The Willkür is free to reject the moral law, not in the sense that it is appropriate that it do so, but in the sense that it is capable of doing so. Indeed, the Willkür must be free to reject the moral law if the notion of normative morality is to make any sense at all. Willkür's being free to reject the moral law does not alter the fact that it is subject to the moral law, however. John Silber writes, ". . . that which violates the laws of reason must be subject to them . . ."[25] I think that Silber is right about this, although it may not be altogether obvious from what he actually says. The crux of the issue lies in the use of the term 'violation'. If the Willkür were not subject to the moral law, then it would not make sense to call a failure to act in accordance with the moral law a 'violation'. The faculty of choice, as free, is subject to the moral law, but there follows from this no guarantee that morally appropriate actions will result.

C. Kant's Concept of a 'Holy Will' and Its Importance for an Understanding of the Distinction Between Wille and Willkür.

Although I have not finished characterizing the two different senses of 'will', it seems important to turn to some discussion of Kant's concept of a 'holy will' at this point. One cannot adequately analyze the attributes of the two senses of 'will' without first entering upon this digression.

Kant's use of the concept of a 'holy will' is notoriously unclear. It is not obvious what Kant understands as the function of the concept, nor is it clear exactly what the nature of the concept is. Fortunately enough for Kant, his whole moral theory does not seem to rise or fall on this one notion, but it is nevertheless important to analyze the concept of a 'holy will', and to determine its function in his moral theory, especially since doing so throws some light on the distinction between two senses of 'will'.

The simplest, most straightforward way to interpret the holy will would seem to be to construe it as a paradigm case of a good will. That is, it appears at first glance to make sense to understand the holy will as an ideal towards which

19

we should strive in our actions. I think that, while Kant may intend for the holy will to serve this purpose in a rough way at the point where it enters the discussion in the Grundlegung, the concept of a holy will can serve such a purpose at most only in a formal sense, and never in a dynamic way. Let me elaborate these claims.

Kant introduces the concept of a holy will in Section II of the Grundlegung, at the beginning of his general discussion of kinds of imperatives.[26] He speaks of the holy will as a perfectly good will:

> A perfectly good will, therefore, would be equally subject to objective laws (of the good), but it could not be conceived as constrained by them to act in accord with them, because, according to its own subjective constitution, it can be determined to act only through the conception of the good. Thus no imperatives hold for the divine will or, more generally, for a holy will. The 'ought' is here out of place, for the volition of itself is necessarily in unison with the law.[27]

That Kant refers to the holy will here as a 'perfectly good will' is one rather obvious sign that he intends for the concept to serve as a model or paradigm. A second, more circumstantial indication that Kant intends for the concept of a holy will to serve as a paradigm is its placement in the text, at the beginning of his discussion of imperatives. That is, it seems reasonable to suppose from its placement that the holy will is being offered as a model which the categorical imperative admonishes us to approximate.

Now, if Kant indeed intends that the concept of a 'holy will' should serve the kind of

20

purpose I have outlined, there remains the question as to whether in fact the concept can serve such a purpose. The answer to this depends upon the way in which one understands the notion of a 'model' or 'paradigm'. In a formal sense, the 'holy will', given that its volition is always in accordance with the moral law, can serve quite well as a paradigm. In a dynamic sense, however, when we consider the *way* in which the 'holy will' would choose (if this is the right word for what the 'holy will' does) to follow the moral law, the concept of a 'holy will' cannot possibly serve as a model. The reason why it cannot has very much to do with the concept of constraint (Nötigung, in German). The German verb nötigen, from which Nötigung is derived, has several possible translations, including: 'to necessitate'; 'to compel'; 'to force'; 'to determine'; and, in Beck's translation of the Grundlegung, 'to constrain'. It is obvious from the derivation of Nötigung from the verb nötigen that 'constraint' is taken by Kant to be an active concept, which should be thought of as an act of compelling or constraining oneself to act in accordance with a certain principle, namely the moral law. Kant calls constraint the, ". . . relation of an objective law of reason to a will which is not in its subjective constitution necessarily determined by this law."[28] That moral constraint must be an act of self-constraint follows from what Kant says about the principle of autonomy. We shall see more about this later.

It should be noted that the notion of 'constraint' itself is broader than merely moral constraint. Even in the case of hypothetical imperatives, we have to be able to explain how the will can be constrained to act in accordance with such imperatives. As Kant writes,

> The question now arises: how are all these imperatives possible? This question does not require

21

an answer as to how the action
which the imperative commands can
be performed but merely as to how
the constraint of the will, which
the imperative expresses in the
problem, can be conceived.[29]

Kant argues, of course, that the only kind of imperative which presents anything of a problem so far as the constraint question is concerned is the imperative of morality, the categorical imperative.

It is of the essence of action having moral worth, in human beings, that one constrain or coerce oneself to act in a certain way, and from a certain motive. Indeed, it is the notion of constraint that makes the 'ought' applicable in the case of human beings, whereas it is not applicable in the case of the holy will. The function of a moral paradigm, in the dynamic sense, is to provide a model to which one might point and say, 'If you would be moral, do as he does'. But, in point of fact, it is impossible for human beings to act as the holy will does. For the holy will acts as it does without benefit of constraint, and constraint is essential to the moral worth of actions in human beings.

I do not mean to be suggesting that one must, in performing an action having moral worth, always 'tear oneself away' from something which one desires. Kant is quite clear in noting that there are some duties to which we also have direct inclination. Nevertheless, one must constrain oneself in two ways in performing such actions: (1) one must constrain oneself to do the action rather than not (the action does not follow necessarily from its presentation as good); (2) one must constrain oneself to perform the action from a motive of duty rather than from a motive of inclination. This latter sense of constraint must be possible, for otherwise one could never perform an action of moral worth to which one also had an inclination, and this is surely not Kant's position on the matter (although it is to be admitted that there is disagreement among commentators on this point).

There is yet further evidence that the concept of a holy will cannot function as a paradigm case of a moral being. It seems impossible, in Kantian terms, to say that a holy will acts morally at all. Kant writes, "Morality, therefore, consists in the relation of every action to that legislation through which alone a realm of ends is possible."[30] I understand 'legislation', as Kant uses the notion, to be a two-party relation which necessarily involves constraint. If this analysis of legislation is correct, then the holy will cannot serve as a moral paradigm, because constraint, and therefore legislation, are not applicable to the holy will. I shall discuss Kant's concept of legislation in more detail in a later chapter.

To summarize, what we have seen here is that there are really two quite different senses in which the concept of a holy will might be said to serve as a model of how to act. In a purely formal sense, the holy will can serve as a model, in that its actions are, indeed, always in accord with the moral law. Its maxims (if it can be said to have 'maxims' at all) would therefore be examples of principles which could be universalized. In the more substantive dynamic sense, though, the holy will cannot serve as a model, because a holy will is never presented with the kind of situation in which constraint in either of the two senses I have mentioned is required. The moral task for human beings is to constrain themselves to follow the dictates of the moral law, and no guidance along this line can possibly be forthcoming from the holy will.

Let us return again to the concept of the 'holy will' itself, and see what may be learned from it, regarding Kant's concept of the will in general. It has already been noted that duty does not apply to a holy will, because the holy will does not have the alternatives of choice that make the notion of duty applicable to it.[31] The moral perfection of a holy will, then, evidently lies in its being able to choose only that which is required by morality.[32]

Indeed, it is not even clear that it is reasonable to say that a holy will acts or chooses at all, in any significant sense. In order to choose, the holy will must, of course, have a faculty of choice, and it is less than obvious that Kant thinks it does. In any event, it is clear that even if the holy will does have a faculty of choice, it is of a nature quite different from that of the Willkür of human beings. In the first Critique, Kant writes, of the human faculty of choice,

> . . . a will is sensuous, in so far as it is *pathologically affected*, i.e., by sensuous motives; it is *animal (arbitrium brutum)*, if it can be pathologically *necessitated*. The human will is certainly an *arbitrium sensitivum*, not, however, *brutum*, but *liberum*.[33]

What Kant has done here is, apparently, to treat the Willkür *(arbitrium sensitivum)* as a generic term under which two species are subsumed, *arbitrium brutum* (animal will) and *arbitrium liberum* (human will).

It is the designation of Willkür as *arbitrium sensitivum* that makes it somewhat questionable whether the holy will could be said to have a faculty of choice at all. That is, the use of the term *sensitivum* in this connection could be taken as suggesting that Kant understands the notion of a faculty of choice *per se* as having an essentially pathological component, or an essentially sensuous component. If this is the case, then the holy will, since it is totally cut off from sensuous inclinations, cannot be said to have choice at all.

But it is not altogether obvious that Kant intended that the faculty of choice be thought of

24

as having an essentially sensuous component. He writes, ". . . a will is sensuous, so far as it is *pathologically affected* . . ."[34] Kant does not say, however, that a will must be sensuous in order to have a faculty of choice at all. Had Kant wished to say this, he could certainly have done so. The fact that he did not explicitly limit the Willkür by including an essentially sensuous component does not prove that Kant would not assent to such a limitation, of course, and thus the evidence on this issue seems somewhat mixed. It is clear that, if the holy will can be said to have a faculty of choice at all, this would be a faculty of choice that is not subject to any pathological affectation whatever.

It is possible, I think, to view Kant's concept of a 'holy will' as analogous to Aristotle's notion of a prime or unmoved mover. I am not at all sure of the extent to which Kant would accept such a comparison, but it is nevertheless illuminating to see how Aristotle might account for the actions of a holy will.

Aristotle writes, ". . . since that which is moved and moves is intermediate, there is something which moves without being moved, . . . And the object of desire and the object of thought move in this way; they move without being moved."[35] And, further, ". . . the final cause is (a) some being for whose good an action is done, and (b) something at which the action aims; and of these the latter exists among unchangeable entities though the former does not."[36]

If we grant that choosing involves movement - some change in oneself - then, if it is possible for the holy will to be thought of as unmoved, it must be the case that the holy will does not choose. Since choice is an essential component in human action for Kant, it would then follow that the holy will does not 'act' in the way in which human beings do.

Viewing the holy will as a final cause,

25

something at which human action aims, might give it a function in Kant's theory, were it not for two points: (1) this would seem, on its face, to be in violation of the principle of autonomy; (2) Kant says of the holy will, ". . . it can be *determined to act* only through the conception of the good."[37] This passage seems to suggest that Kant thinks of the holy will as acting, and not as being merely that for the sake of which someone acts.

It is, I think, the distinction between <u>Wille</u> and <u>Willkür</u> that is the key to understanding the significance of Aristotle's unmoved mover for Kant's position, at least so far as the human will is concerned. The human will is, for Kant, both moved and unmoved. That is, the <u>Wille</u> is a spontaneous source of legislation for the maxims of action and is essentially unmoved - it is, as Kant says, neither free nor unfree;[38] the <u>Willkür</u> is both mover and moved. Thus I think that, though Kant might not accept an analysis of the holy will as being entirely like Aristotle's unmoved mover, there is an analysis of the human will, relying upon the crucial distinction between the two senses of 'will', for which Aristotle's notion is quite illuminating. I shall discuss this point in more detail later, in the chapter on the will as a 'causality'.

D. The Concept of 'Choice'.

Some brief general remarks regarding the concept of 'choice' are in order here. I am speaking now of the notion of a choice itself, and not particularly about the faculty of choice. There are many points relevant to such a discussion, but I shall concentrate here only on the relevance of the positions of Leibniz and Aristotle for an understanding of Kant's views.

1. Kant and Leibniz.

Leibniz employs the concept of a 'wise being' which functions, I think, very much like Kant's

26

concept of a holy will. Leibniz writes,

> We must also distinguish be-
> tween a *necessity* which takes
> place because the opposite im-
> plies a contradiction (which
> necessity is called *logical*,
> *metaphysical*, or *mathematical*),
> and a necessity which is *moral*,
> whereby a wise being chooses the
> best, and every mind follows the
> strongest inclination.[39]

Setting aside for the moment the obvious fact
that Kant might be troubled by Leibniz' reference to 'every mind following the strongest
inclination', I think that the significance of
the somewhat tenuous analogy between Kant and
Leibniz on this point is that it shows a tradition of thinking of a holy will (or 'wise
being') as having the capacity for choice.

   There are, of course, problems with the conception of 'choice' involved here. Leibniz' use
of the notion of a 'wise being' who must choose
the best helps, it may be thought, to illustrate
how such a 'wise being' (God, perhaps?) might be
conceived as choosing at all. Leibniz' God chooses
to create the best of all possible universes, and
could not have chosen to create a possible world
that is less than the best. But, since there is
really only one world that it is possible for God
to create, why call this a 'choice' at all? I
think that the point is that the concept of a
choice is necessary to make sense of any action's
being initiated, even if the choice is not a choice
among alternatives in any meaningful sense, and
really serves only as a 'logical placeholder' to
mark the place where deliberation ends and action
begins. Even if God has no option but to create
this particular world, He must nevertheless do the
task, and set the action into motion. In this regard, if we think of God as being actively involved
in the creation of the world, we are clearly

thinking of Him as an efficient cause of the world, and not merely as a final cause, to continue to employ Aristotle's terminology.[40] It is not equally obvious, thought, that we are thereby thinking of God as being moved, rather than unmoved. We shall return to this point later, in the chapter on the 'causality' of the will, and I think it might create more confusion than clarity to explore it further here.

It is this sense of 'choice' as the starting-point of action that seems applicable to the concept of a holy will. I know of no place in Kant's works where he gives a name to a sense of *arbitrium* that belongs to a holy will, but I conclude that it is consistent with his position that there be such a sense.

2. Kant and Aristotle.

A brief reference to Aristotle's concept of 'choice' may help to bring Kant's own position into perspective. Aristotle writes, ". . . choice involves a rational principle and thought"[41] Further,

> The same thing is deliberated upon
> and is chosen, except that the ob-
> ject of choice is already determi-
> nate, since it is that which has
> been decided upon as the result of
> deliberation that is the object of
> choice . . . The object of choice
> being one of the things in our power
> which is desired after deliberation,
> choice will be the deliberate de-
> sire of things in our own power;[42]

Finally, Aristotle notes that we must ultimately choose at some point if anything is to happen, for "If we are to be always deliberating, we shall have to go on to infinity."[43]

We should note, somewhat parenthetically, that Aristotle's concepts of deliberation and choice are close to the common-sense notions to

28

which we generally refer in our ordinary speech.
That is, he views choice as choice among alternatives, and deliberation as among alternatives,
rather than seeing these concepts as mere 'logical placeholders' in a theory of action. That
this is the case is clear from the following:
"The object of choice being *one of the things*
in our own power which is desired *after deliberation*, choice will be deliberate desire of
things in our power."[44] I think that Kant's primary concern is with human choice, which is choice
among alternatives, though it seems that there is
reason to believe that Kant also subscribes to a
concept of choice, in the case of the holy will,
which serves only a 'placeholder' function. This
'placeholder' function applies in both cases,
though the notion of real alternatives pertains
only to the human will.

It seems that, for Aristotle, *choice* is the
end-product of a process of deliberation. And, in
so far as human actions are concerned, we must
choose if we are to act at all. It is important
to note here that some of theoccurrences that I
might ordinarily term 'actions' of mine would not
fit the precise description Aristotle sets down.
For example, if I act in a blind rage, and do not
deliberate about what I am going to do, this could
not constitute an 'action' in the fullest sense of
the term. Nevertheless, there are occasions on
which we, and Aristotle as well, would say that
we were responsible for these occurrences, even
though we could not term them 'actions' in the
fullest sense.

I think that this difficulty need not detain
us. The main point to see is that choice is, for
Aristotle, the end-product of a chain of deliberation. Notice now a passage from Kant:

> The faculty of desiring in accord-
> ance with concepts is called the
> faculty of doing or forebearing as
> one likes . . . insofar as the ground

29

> determining it to action is found
> in the faculty of desire itself,
> and not in the object. Insofar
> as it is combined with the con-
> sciousness of the capacity of its
> action to produce its object, it
> is called *will*, or *Choice* [*Willkür*].[45]

The similarities between Kant and Aristotle
are clear: Kant speaks of 'desiring in accordance with concepts', and Aristotle of choice as
involving 'a rational principle and thought';
Kant refers to the ground of action being found
within the faculty of desire, and Aristotle
writes, "It seems, then, as has been said, that
man is a moving principle of actions"[46];

There thus appear to be two senses of 'choice'
at work here. In one sense, surely the one we
usually have in mind in our ordinary speech,
'choice' refers to the having of real alternatives.
In the other sense, however, the concept of a
'choice' performs a kind of logical function within the concept of action. Even if a holy will cannot do anything other than the right thing, it
must nevertheless do the right thing, and choice
is the 'logical vehicle', as it were, whereby the
action is initiated.

Let us leave the discussion of the logical
function of the concept of choice, and speak more
about real choices. In the ordinary sense, saying that one 'chooses' may mean several different
things. It may mean this: one wants ice cream,
and can have either chocolate or vanilla. Or, one
might mean that one has to decide whether to spend
one's money on an expensive dinner, or on tickets
to the theater. The decision here is between two
things one happens to want, but, unlike the previous example, the choice here is between two
different kinds of things, at least in a limited
sense. To be more precise, I should say that the
choice is between different 'kinds' of things in
the following restricted sense: having dinner

and going to the theater are things of the same
kind in the sense that they are both things
which would satisfy one's desires; they are
different, of course, in ways in which different
flavors of ice cream are not. But there is a
final sense of 'having an alternative' which
is stronger than either of these two senses:
in the strongest possible sense of the phrase,
'having an alternative' would mean having to
choose between something that one desired to do
and something that one believed that one ought
to do. Aristotle, of course, is of the view
that the ideal in humans is to come to a state
of doing the right thing through 'force of habit,'
so that the conflict between what one wants, and
what one feels one ought to do disappears.

Let us pursue this last point further. Aristotle writes, "Virtue, then, being of two kinds,
intellectual and moral, intellectual virtue in
the main owes both its birth and its growth to
teaching . . . while moral virtue comes about as
a result of habit,"[47] And, further, "Neither by
nature, then, nor contrary to nature do the virtues arise in us; rather we are adapted by nature
to receive them, and are made perfect by habit."[48]

Several comments are relevant here. First of
all, we should note that it seems intuitively peculiar to say that virtue is the result of habit.
To act out of 'habit', we would ordinarily suppose,
is to act without thinking about what one is doing.
Secondly, Kant's position seems, on its face, to
be in open conflict with Aristotle's, since Kant
emphasizes the notion of constraint in his discussion of the relation of the human will to the
moral law.[49] Now, I think that it is neither the
case that Aristotle's position is so counter-in-
tuitive as his use of the term 'habit' might lead
us to think, nor that Kant and Aristotle are so
far apart as they appear. This latter point is
particularly important to understanding Kant's
use of the concept of constraint.

What does Aristotle mean in saying that moral

virtue is the result of 'habit'? In discussing
what it means for an agent to be 'virtuous',
Aristotle writes, ". . . his action must proceed
from a firm and unchangeable character."50 The
way one gets into this 'firm and unchangeable
character' is by performing virtuous acts for
their own sakes. Since the very performance of
actions involves, for Aristotle, deliberation
and choice, it can hardly be the case that one
would perform a virtuous act without thinking.
One need only look at the first two criteria of
acting virtuously to see this: ". . . in the
first place he must have knowledge, secondly,
he must choose the acts, and choose them for
their own sakes."51

What, then, is to be said of the relation
between Kant and Aristotle on this point? It is
Aristotle's view that one can come to have a 'firm
and unchangeable character' with regard to acting
in a certain way. Is this contrary to what Kant
says about constraint? Let us examine Kant's remarks once again:

> . . . if reason of itself does
> not sufficiently determine the
> will, andif the will is subju-
> gated to subjective conditions
> (certain incentives) which do not
> always agree with objective con-
> ditions; in a word, if the will
> is not of itself in complete
> accord with reason (the actual
> case of men), then the actions
> which are recognized as object-
> ively necessary are subjectively
> contingent, and the determination
> of such a will according to ob-
> jective laws is constraint.52

Are we to think from this that Kant sees the business of acting morally as a constant struggle in
which the will engages? Must I think of myself
as constantly torn between inclination and duty?

That this is not Kant's view is clear:

> It is far more difficult to note
> this difference [between acting
> from duty and acting from incli-
> nation] when the action is in
> accordance with duty and, in
> addition, the subject has a direct
> inclination to do it.[53]

And, further, ". . . it is a duty to preserve one's
life, and, moreover, everyone has a direct inclination to do so."[54] Thus, in Kant's view, it is
not always the case that our desires and our duty
are in conflict. Nor does it seem to be the case
that, where desire and duty are in conflict, that
there is some kind of internal war going on, in
which one must struggle with oneself, wrestle with
oneself as to what to do. One could, consistently
with Kant's position, accustom oneself to habit-
ually apply constraint, so that, in a particular
case, one might experience no difficulty, no tor-
ment, in following the dictates of the moral law.
On Aristotle's side, it seems clear that he considers us still to be influenced by our passions,
even if we have come to be able to control them:
". . . we are neither praised nor blamed for our
passions . . . but for our virtues and our vices
we *are* praised or blamed."[55] Aristotle's point
is that the truly virtuous person is one who is
in complete control of his or her passions - not
one who has ceased to have passions. This is
surely compatible with Kant's position. We can
imagine a human being acting with perfect constraint: this would be a person who, in fact,
always followed the dictates of the moral law;
what we cannot imagine is a human being who is
not under constraint, for the need for constraint
is, for Kant, a part of the human condition, and
a will which was not under constraint would simply
not be 'human' at all.

To return for a moment to the discussion of
the holy will, it seems that we must say that the
Willkür of a holy will, if indeed it has a faculty

33

of choice at all, must be so constituted that its only alternative as a determining ground of its maxims is the moral law.[56] A maxim is, for Kant, a subjective principle of action. The determining ground of a subjective principle of action is the factor or consideration which decides whether something will be a principle of action at all. That is, if we are asked whether a particular maxim is possible, we cannot really answer without first knowing what the determining ground is to be in the case under consideration. To be a determining ground of maxims is to be a guiding principle of that faculty which selects maxims, namely, the faculty of choice. The determining ground is, in short, one's reason for adopting a given maxim.

3. Choice and the Human Willkür.

    The notion of a 'reason for acting' leads to an interesting discussion of the concept of choice as it applies to the human will. It seems that we should say that there are two possible levels of choice for the Willkür: (1) choices as to what to do in particular instances; (2) choices as to what to take as the determining ground for choices in particular instances. There are two important questions to be asked about these two levels of choice: (1) are these two levels of choice applicable to Willkür *per se*, or only to the human faculty of choice; (2) when these two levels of choice are present in a faculty of choice, what relationship exists between the two levels? By analyzing these two levels of choice and their inter-relation, we shall gain a clearer understanding of Kant's concept of Willkür.

    As a parenthetical note before beginning a more detailed discussion of the two levels of choice, I think it is the case that Kant would consider the distinction between the two levels to be a logical distinction, rather than a real one. That is, Kant would not 'reify' the distinction between the two levels of choice. His view on this point seems

34

analogous to his position regarding the relation between empirical and non-empirical apperception, or 'self-consciousness'.[57]

I think that the level of choice which is common to animal and human faculties of choice is the first level, namely, that of deciding what to do in particular instances (since the holy will may or may not have a faculty of choice with real choices to make, I will henceforth omit it from the discussion). Dogs and men both make 'decisions' as to what to do in concrete cases. It is probably a bit misleading to speak in this way, since dogs clearly do not 'choose' in the same fashion as persons. We have already seen how Kant's view of choice parallels that of Aristotle, involving for each the employment of reason.[58] Whatever else we might say of dogs, Kant would surely say that we cannot know them to be rational.

The second level of choice, however, seems appropriate only to the human will. That is, it is only the human faculty of choice that is presented with alternative kinds of reasons for doing things. Animals are not subject to the demands of the moral law (so far as we know, at any rate), and therefore cannot choose to take the moral law as a reason for doing something. The human faculty of choice, because it is subject both to the passions and to the moral law, has to choose between them. Of the human will, Lewis Beck has written:

> Man is the only being in the world that can get himself entangled in these paradoxes, . . . For man is the only being in the world who is a citizen of two worlds, and subject both to psychological explanation and moral exhortation; he is the only being in the world who is torn between the roles of spectator and actor . . . If he were a beast, he could neither create nor

35

obey laws; were he a god, he
could create them without having
to obey but could not create laws.
But he is, for good or evil, neither
beast nor slave nor God.[59]

Let us now examine the relationship between
the two levels of choice within the human will,
keeping in mind that Kant does not intend to 'reify' the distinction between the levels. There
are several questions to be posed at this juncture:
(1) is one level of choice in any sense logically
prior to the other; (2) do the different levels
of choice ever occur independently of one another,
that is, does one ever find, in the human faculty
of choice, a choice of a particular action that
does not involve at the same time the selection
of the reason for pursuing the course of action,
or a choice of a reason for acting not involving
the choice of a particular action. The question
of the 'reification' of the two levels of choice
is relevant to the answers to these questions.

Since, as I have said, Kant would not 'reify'
the distinction between the two levels of choice,
it seems clear that the two levels of choice do
not occur independently of one another. Thus,
the second question about the two levels of choice
would appear to resolve rather easily, and in the
negative. But let us not dismiss this question
too lightly: can one ever be said to choose a
motive for acting without choosing a particular
maxim, which is the context within which one chooses
a motive? There does seem to be a sense in which
one can speak of choosing a motive alone. That is,
we do frequently speak of 'setting oneself to do
the right thing', and this in advance of having
any particular context in mind. This might be
seen as choosing a motive in the absence of a particular setting. I think, though, that Kant would
find the notion of a choice of motive thus abstracted
from the choice of a particular maxim of action to
be, at best, morally uninteresting.

Kant writes, "Morality, therefore, consists

36

in the relation of every action to that legislation through which alone a realm of ends
is possible."[60]   If Kant's concern is with
actions, which are related to maxims, he will
not be particularly concerned with what we might
term 'pure policy decisions', or the choice of
motives in the absence of a concrete situation.
That is, one's willingness to act out of a certain motivation can only be demonstrated in concrete situations in which one in fact acts out
of a certain motivation. All of this seems to
be true, regardless of what one thinks of the
stand Kant takes on the possibility of ever
knowing the true nature of one's motive in any
particular instance. The logic of choice is,
as it were, one thing, and the epistemology of
choice is quite another. I shall say more about
these matters later.

On this particular point, Kant's position
is not unlike that of Jean-Paul Sartre, who writes,

> If man, as the existentialist con-
> ceives him, is indefinable, it is
> because at first he is nothing.
> Only afterward will he be something,
> and he himself will have made what
> he will be . . . Not only is man
> what he conceives himself to be,
> but he is also only what he wills
> himself to be *after* this thrust
> toward existence.[61]

I take Sartre to be committed to the view that one's
claims to be willing to act in certain ways or for
certain reasons can be demonstrated only through
one's actions. For Kant, too, the proof of one's
commitment can come only in action - though, for
Kant, the motive for action remains hidden.

Those who find comparisons of Kant and Sartre
unseemly will perhaps prefer a comparison with Aristotle. On the subject of becoming just and tem-
perate, Aristotle writes,

37

> . . . if the acts that are in
> accordance with the virtues have
> themselves a certain character it
> does not follow that they are done
> justly or temperately. The agent
> must be in a certain condition
> when he does them; in the first
> place he must have knowledge, sec-
> ondly he must choose the acts, and
> choose them for their own sakes,
> and thirdly his action must pro-
> ceed from a firm and unchangeable
> character.[63]

While Aristotle would claim that, once one had
acquired such a 'firm and unchangeable character',
it makes a manner of sense to speak of one as
being of that character even when one is not acting, several things are clear: (1) the effect
of this 'firm and unchangeable character' upon
the world manifests itself only in particular
actions; (2) one comes to be of such a character
only by electing repeatedly to perform virtuous
acts for their own sake. Surely, Kant would
share Aristotle's position on these points.

The point of this brief digression has been
to show why Kant would find the notion of 'pure
policy decisions' morally uninteresting. Despite
this, there are still important questions to be
raised regarding the relations between the choice
of particular maxims and the choice of the moral
law as the supreme guiding principle in the selection of maxims. Having just said that Kant is
not interested in 'pure policy decisions', it may
seem strange to return to the relation between
the two levels of choice. But this is really not
so strange at all. Kant is certainly interested
in 'policy decisions', insofar as they involve
the question of the motives for one's actions.
But there is a difference between concrete choices
and abstract ones - that I have termed 'pure policy decisions'. It is the later sort of 'policy
decision' that Kant would find uninteresting -
he is clearly quite interested in the former.

Indeed, Kant's entire doctrine of the
moral worth of actions rests on the election
of the moral law as one's motive. Kant writes,
". . . to have moral worth an action must be
done from duty . . . Duty is the necessity of
an action executed from respect for law."[64] It
is clear that, when Kant refers to acting 'from
respect for law', he is speaking of one's motive for acting.

Kant's actual position regarding the nature
of the relation between the selection of the moral
law as the guiding principle of maxims and the
appropriateness of maxims is unclear, but there
is some reason to think that Kant does not recognize this relationship as a problem. He writes,

> . . . a critical examination of
> pure practical reason is not of
> such extreme importance as that
> of speculative reason, because
> human reason, even in the common-
> est mind, can easily be brought
> to a high degree of correctness
> and completeness in moral matters.[65]

I take Kant as saying that persons know, for the
most part, full well what they ought to do, and
do not stand in need of much instruction, beyond
the normal moral education that one receives from
living in society. In the present context, we
might say that, while morally appropriate maxims
do not follow inevitably from the selection of the
moral law as the determining ground of maxims,
such maxims would follow to a very large extent.
In any event, once an agent had taken care in exam-
ining his or her situation, and had made a serious
effort to formulate a maxim that would accord with
the requirements of the moral law, we would surely
conclude that the agent had done all that could
possibly be required.

We should turn now to the question whether
one of the two levels of choice is logically prior
to the other, but, before doing so, I should make

39

one point of clarification. It is important
not to confuse the second level of choice, the
choice of motive with what R. M. Hare terms
'decisions of principle'.[66] One might decide
not to say something because it was false, and
this involves an implicit decision of principle -
namely, the decision to abide by the principle
of not saying things that one knows or takes to
be false, or of not doing so in circumstances
like those in which one finds oneself at the
moment. But the kind of choice I refer to here
is quite different. One might adopt the principle of not saying that which one knows or
takes to be false for either of the two sorts
of reasons open to the human will. That is,
one could adopt the principle of never saying
that which one knows to be false out of fear
that one would otherwise be ostracized by the
community, or one could adopt the same principle because one took it to be morally obligatory
to refrain from saying that which one knows to
be false. I do not think that the distinction
I make here between two different kinds of reasons
for acting on a certain principle is at all inconsistent with Hare's position. I wish only to emphasize the difference between Hare's discussion
and the distinction I have drawn. As we shall see
later, Kant's analysis of the will as a 'causality'
is relevant to the present concerns.

To deal adequately with the question of the
logical priority of one sense of choice over the
other, it is necessary to engage first in a brief
digression regarding Kant's use of the concept of
a 'maxim'. It seems that Kant uses the notion in
more than one sense, and this can give rise to some
confusion. This ought not to be damaging to the
main lines of Kant's position, so long as we are
alert to the fact and guard against confusing the
senses of 'maxim'.

It appears that Kant's concept of a 'maxim',
in the fullest sense of the term, includes within
it a reference to the agent's reason for acting.
A maxim is, . . . the subjective principle of

40

acting and . . . contains the practical rule
which reason determines according to the conditions of the subject . . ."[67] In discussing
his notorious four examples of maxims which are
alleged to involve violations of duty, Kant says
"His maxim, however, is: *For love of myself*, I
make it my principle . . ."[68] The reference to
the reason for acting ('for love of myself')
here is clear.

Given that, as we have just seen, Kant's concept of a maxim contains a reference to the
agent's motive for acting, it would seem that
the choice of motive is at least logically implicit in the choice of any particular maxim.
This is, of course, not to say that one can know
what any particular agent's motive is at any particular time. As Kant writes,

> It is in fact absolutely im-
> possible by experience to dis-
> cern with complete certainty a
> single case in which the maxim
> of an action, however much it
> may conform to duty, rested sole-
> ly on moral grounds and on the
> conception of one's duty.[69]

Nor is any of this to say that Kant views the selection of a motive to be something that occurs
independently of the choice of a particular
course of action.

We should pause here to take account of what
seems to be a certain inconsistency in Kant's use
of the term 'maxim'. While the examples he gives
of maxims which are contrary to duty would tend to
indicate that Kant thinks of the motive to action
as being a part of the maxim itself, there are
places where he uses the term 'maxim' in a way
that suggests a distinction between the 'content'
of the maxim and its motivational component.
Thus, while it seems that, on the one hand, the
motive is an integral part of any maxim, it also

seems to be the case that, at least in certain instances, the motive and the 'content' of the maxim are independent of one another. That is, the 'content' of the maxim will remain the same, whether the motive for action be duty or inclination. This is the case with actions that accord with duty and to which we also have direct inclination. For instance, consider Kant's example of a merchant who gives honest treatment to a customer. The action is in accord with duty, regardless of why it is done, but has moral worth only if done from a motive of duty. But, though the action has no moral worth when done from a motive of self-interest, Kant still wishes to say that the 'maxim' is in accord with duty. Does this apparent inconsistency in the usage of the term 'maxim' cause problems for Kant? I think not. He makes a clear distinction between the permissibility of an action and the praiseworthiness of an action. The key to seeing this lies in understanding the distinction between the 'content' of a maxim and its motivational component.

In the passage cited above, Kant seems to be saying specifically that one cannot discern the motive behind a particular action. I think, though, that Kant would also have to agree that one cannot discern the maxim itself with any certainty, either. This is the case, not only because the motive is a part of the maxim (in one of the senses in which Kant uses that term), but also because it seems possible to describe any action whatever as falling under a number of maxims.[70] By this, I mean not merely the sort of case just mentioned, in which a merchant may give honest service from a motive of duty or from a motive of self-interest. It is also possible to describe the action being performed as falling under any number of different maxims. For example, Al Capone's actions in running organized crime in Chicago might have been described as 'committing murder and mayhem', or as 'attempting

42

to earn a living'. One maxim passes the test of
moral permissibility, while the other fails,
rather grotesquely, I should say. I have no wish
at this point to enter upon a full-scale discussion
of the problem of act-descriptions in connection
with Kant's work. I want to note primarily that
the existence of this difficulty is evidence for
the claim that, for Kant, it is not possible to
discern with certainty what any person's maxim of
action is at any given time.

4.   The Problem of Alternative Act-Descriptions.

    Before leaving the question of alternative
act-descriptions altogether, however, let us at
least take note of some of the secondary literature on the subject. Two works are especially
relevant to a consideration of this problem: (1)
Acting on Principle, by Onora Nell[71]; (2) Generalization in Ethics, by Marcus G. Singer.[72]
Let us see how the problem of alternative or competing act-descriptions is to be characterized.
Professor Nell writes,

> Not only can a given princi-
> ple be acted on repeatedly and
> in various ways, but any given
> act exemplifies numerous princi-
> ples . . . Of any act and of any
> agent an indefinitely large num-
> ber of descriptions is true.[73]

Of an objection to what he calls the 'generalization argument' - and, given the similarities between Singer's view and Kant's, to Kant's position
as well - Singer says,

> This objection arises out of the
> fact that an act can be described
> in many different ways, that it
> can be, in other words, an instance
> of more than one kind of act. It
> follows from this, so it is argued,
> that depending on the way an act
> is described, the generalization

> argument will lead us to in-
> compatible results, and hence
> can be used to show that the
> act is right and that it is
> wrong.[74]

Singer's remarks show the extent of the trouble
that he and Kant will be in, if the objection can
be made to stick.

Singer's view, of course, is that the charge
does not stick at all, because certain kinds of
'competing' descriptions are themselves defect-
ive, and therefore cannot be used as part of an
objection to the generalization argument. The
two defects mentioned by Singer are what he terms
'invertibility' and 'reiterability', though they
might also have been called making descriptions
too broad and too narrow, respectively. The generalization argument is 'invertible' with respect to a given action, if it is the case that,
though the consequences of everyone's acting in
a certain way would be undesirable, the consequences of no one's acting in that way would be
equally undesirable. In such cases, the generalization argument is not supposed to apply, Singer
says, and therefore the fact that it seems to lead
to absurd consequences when applied to such situations cannot count as an objection. The generalization argument is 'reiterable' with respect
to a given action, if it is the case that the
action is described in such a way as to seize upon
some arbitrary or irrelevant feature of the action,
so as to make it appear that the generalization
argument has absurd consequences. For example, it
might be said that if everyone enrolled in a particular section of a philosophy course the consequences - over-crowding and the like - would be
undesirable, and therefore no one ought to enroll
in that course. While it may seem at times that
students are acting on this principle, the objection is nonetheless invalid. It is invalid,
Singer claims, because the exact same point can be
made about any other section of any other course,

44

and thus the ultimate consequence of the argument would be that no student ought ever to enroll in any course - but this, as any instructor can plainly see, is absurd. Singer's point is that any attempt to invalidate the generalization argument itself by use of such reiterable examples is to be dismissed out-of-hand, because the argument is not meant to have application to such cases, or, perhaps more correctly, to cases thusly described.

There is a problem here, which should be noted in passing. This is, of course, the problem of deciding which features of an act are 'relevant' and which are 'irrelevant' or 'arbitrary'. In part, I think that this depends on one's purposes in describing an act. If one wishes merely to describe an action, and to do so in such detail that the act can be picked out from other members of the same class of actions, then every feature of the act is relevant, or at least potentially so. If, on the other hand, one wishes only to cite the class of actions of which a particular act is an instance, then only certain general features of the act are relevant, the remaining characteristics becoming irrelevant for that purpose of classification.

Act-description for the purposes of moral theory is, for the most part, the same as act-description for the purpose of general classification. Whether a particular act is right or wrong depends, for Singer, partly on whether the class of actions to which the particular act belongs is right or wrong and partly on whether the act has any unique qualities which would make it an exception to whatever holds of the general class to which it belongs. This may sound as if the arbitrary features of the act have suddenly become relevant, but this is not the case. What Singer is suggesting is that certain characteristics of an act which may serve to separate it from a broader class of acts may also serve to place it in another class of actions whose moral

45

status is different from that of the original class.

This is all well and good, but it assumes something that is less than obvious. If one wants to make an exception of one's own case in an instance of an action which is generally wrong, one must find something about one's own act which excuses it from the general prohibition on acts of that sort. To do this, it appears that one would have to be able to locate some specific individual for whom the act would be wrong, and show that one's own case differed in some significant respect. But, Singer's analysis does not appear capable of isolating on specific individuals in this way. Singer speaks rather obscurely about the 'general grounds' on which actions are right or wrong, but I do not see how this helps.[75] If we are dealing with a case in which each and every instance of an act had undesirable consequences, we could then select any individual at random and use that person as a test case against which to assess one's own situation. But this won't do, for two reasons: (1) if it is really the case that each and every instance of a class of actions is wrong, the, to the extent that one's own action is an instance of that kind of action at all, it is wrong, period, and there is no excusing it - or, rather, the only excuse would be that one's own act is simply not an instance of the prohibited class, that one's act is suffering from a case of 'mistaken identity', as it were; (2) Singer intends for his argument to apply, in principle, to cases in which not each and every instance has undesirable consequences, and here, it seems to me, he simply fails to provide adequate criteria of relevance.[76]

Apart from the difficulty of criteria of relevance, does Singer's analysis really solve the problem of competing act-descriptions? While it surely rules out some of the troublesome cases, it is far from clear that it eliminates all difficulties. Recall our earlier example about Al Capone:

46

describing his actions as 'committing murder and mayhem' obviously would lead to his being condemned, either by Kant's categorical imperative or by Singer's generalization argument. But what of the description of Capone's actions as 'earning a living'? If this description is such that the generalization argument is either invertible or reiterable with respect to it, then the description is illegitimate. But it is not clear that the description has either of these problems. It is certainly not reiterable, since it makes no reference to any of the specifics of Capone's activities, and thus cannot be charged with having selected some arbitrary and irrelevant characteristics of the action. One might say that whether or not Capone earns a living by pursuing his various activities is irrelevant to the case, but this is not the way Singer discusses reiterability, and I think it would beg precisely the question about criteria of relevance standing in need of an answer in any case. Nor does the example appear to be invertible. While some economists may argue that a certain amount of unemployment may sometimes be necessary to cool inflation, I doubt whether anyone would maintain seriously that the consequences of everyone's earning a living would be undesirable, or that the consequences of no one's earning a living would be as desirable as everyone's doing so. We seem to need more analysis.

Onora Nell notes that there may be a way of extricating ourselves from the dilemma in which we are left by Singer's analysis. She suggests that David Lyons' method of generating a '*complete* morally relevant description' of an act might be used.[77] The difficulty with this is that, to adopt Lyons' procedure, one must also adopt some form of utilitarian principle. But, since neither Singer nor Kant will have any of that, this exit seems closed to them.

Professor Nell's work pursues the problem of relevant descriptions in much more detail than I intend to pursue it here. Before leaving the issue altogether, though, I would like to make several

47

final remarks on the subject. Professor Nell suggests that, ". . . Kant provides at least a partial solution to the problem of relevant descriptions when he applies his universality test to agents' maxims."[78] This is an important point, but I do not think that it ultimately solves anything. It is important to be aware that Kant's moral theory has the individual agent and his or her moral deliberations as the primary focus, rather than any attempt to provide us with the means to judge the actions of other people. However, it is not clear how I should conduct myself when I find that there are several ways of thinking about some action I am contemplating, and thus several possible maxims that I might adopt, some permissible, others not. Thus, the observation that Kant applies the universality test to maxims, rather than to actions, does not indicate in itself how the problem of relevant descriptions is to be solved.

But perhaps there is an extension of Professor Nell's observation that will be of some use. How does Kant conceive of maxims as being formulated? This is never made very clear in any of Kant's texts, but I think he sees them as arising somewhat spontaneously in the agent's mind in the process of reacting to some situation. If this is the case, then it makes sense to think of maxims as being presented (or as presenting themselves) to us for consideration. Any agent who, upon seeing that a given maxim was prohibited, went back to see whether the intended action would pass the moral test under some other description could clearly be accused of dealing in bad faith.

5.   The Problem of 'Knowing' One's Maxim.

I will turn now to another sort of problem involved in Kant's employment of the concept of a 'maxim'. This difficulty, that of whether one is ever able to know what one's own maxim is in any particular instance, arises out of the observations made about alternative act-descriptions. I

48

shall argue, ultimately, that the problem is
something of a red herring, so far as Kant's
practical philosophy is concerned. This is
the case because of the differences between
the requirements of theoretical and practical
(moral) certainty.

Let us recall that a maxim is a ". . .
principle according to which the subject acts."[79]
Here, I understand the term 'maxim' in the fullest sense of the term, including both motive and
'content'. Thus, it seems clear that, in the
fullest sense, one cannot be said to have a maxim
for acting without having a motive, and neither
can one be said to 'act' without having a motive.

Let us note now what seems to be a difficulty with Kant's position at this point: if we
cannot discern empirically what anyone's maxim is,
and if this also applies, as it would seem to, to
our own maxims, are we not forced to say that, for
Kant, it is impossible for any individual ever to
know what he or she is doing? And, if it is impossible for one to know what one is doing, is it
not also impossible for one ever to be fully responsible for one's actions? This looks like an
unhappy turn of events. It may appear that Kant's
resolution of this seeming dilemma rests on a distinction between actions which are in accordance
with duty and those which are not. When Kant speaks
of not being able to discern one's motive with certainty, he seems to mean this in application to
cases which are in accordance with duty. Thus, when
the merchant gives honest service to a customer,
no one (including, presumably, the merchant), can
be certain whether the honest service is given out
of duty or out of prudence. Kant does not make
quite the same sort of claim about actions which
are contrary to duty, or, if they are in accord with
duty, are actions to which one has no direct inclination. As he says,

. . . the question does not arise
at all as to whether they may be

49

> carried out *from* duty, since
> they conflict with it . . . it
> is easily decided whether an
> action in accord with duty is
> performed from duty or for some
> selfish purpose. It is far more
> difficult to note this difference
> when the action is in accordance
> with duty and, in addition, the
> subject has a direct inclination
> to do it.[80]

I think that there are grounds for disagreeing with
much of what Kant says on these points. First of
all, I do not see that it is as easy as Kant appears
to think it is to know what the 'content' of one's
maxim is, given what was said above about alternative act-descriptions. If there are difficulties
in knowing what the 'content' of one's maxim is,
then there will also be difficulties in knowing
whether the maxim is in accord with duty or not.
Or, rather, though we may know, in the abstract,
whether a particular maxim is in accord with duty,
we cannot know, in concrete instances, whether it
is in fact our maxim or not. This problem is miti-
gated somewhat if, as I have suggested, it is
Kant's view that maxims arise somewhat spontaneously. If this is the case, then it does seem
possible to know what the 'content' of our maxim
is. But there is a second difficulty. It seems
simply impossible for us to have theoretical knowledge of any agent's motive for action in any particular instance, whether we can know the 'content' of the maxim or not. Indeed, I think that
Kant is simply speaking loosely when he suggests
that one can 'easily' tell whether an action was
done from duty or from some selfish motive. It is
not clear why we should draw a sharp distinction
between 'selfish' motives and 'direct' inclination.

I think, finally, that the problem of knowing
what one is doing in any particular instance remains a real difficulty, so far as theoretical
knowledge is concerned. But all of this may be
beside the point. Kant's moral theory is, after

all, a practical enterprise. To the extent that we can think we are clear as to what we are doing, and as to what our maxim is at any particular time, we can apply Kantian standards to what we take our actions to be. This may sound unsatisfactory but, from a moral point of view, practical certainty is all we have.

Let us relate this portion of our discussion to some remarks made earlier regarding the possibility of choosing a motive in abstraction from the choice of a particular maxim. While, as was said earlier, Kant's views about the way in which maxims arise is not clear, the following should be said: if, as I suggested, maxims (at least their 'content' component - that which the maxim is 'about') arise spontaneously, then we must see the motive to act in accordance with the moral law as serving as part of a 'review board' before which the 'content' of particular maxims must pass. Is this consistent with saying, as I did above, that Kant is not interested in 'pure policy decisions'? I think that it is, because it is still in the process of adopting or rejecting particular maxims that one's stand on the moral law is confirmed. It is only in making the 'content' of particular maxims pass before the 'review board' and in abiding by the 'review board's' judgment that one demonstrates one's commitment to morality.

6. Kant's Moral Epistemology.

It is appropriate here to speak in a preliminary way about the relation between the moral law and particular maxims. There are some formal aspects of the relation which it is important to clarify. The dynamic of this relationship can be explicated only by reference to Kant's conception of the will as a 'causality', and I shall discuss this in some detail later.

On the question of the relation between the moral law and the choice of particular maxims, let us note that the categorical imperative is a formal principle from which no particular principles follow directly. The categorical imperative is therefore always a principle of mediate inference. There is perhaps a sense in which the categorical imperative is like the major premise in a syllogism, telling us, as Beck writes,

> It is a rule like the rules of a syllogism, and just as the rules of a syllogism are empty but tell us what premises are logically necessary in drawing a specific conclusion, or what conclusions follow from given premises, the categorical imperative is a rule for determining what maxims are relevant in making a moral decision.[81]

I find these remarks a bit obscure, but, when Beck says that the categorical imperative determines which maxims are relevant, I presume that he means that we may consider the decision as having been made, and then see which maxims would have served as 'premises' in the making of that decision, or we can consider the maxims as given, and use the categorical imperative to determine what sort of decision is required by the demands of morality. Beck does not mean that the categorical imperative tells us what to do in the absence of any context whatever.

It is obvious that, in the absence of certain factual minor premisses, no particular maxims (decisions) whatever may be inferred from the categorical imperative. Let us explore for a moment the sense in which particular maxims might be said to be 'governed' by the categorical imperative. There are two different schemata suggested by Beck's remarks:

52

A.

    (1)   Act only on a maxim that you can will
          to be universal law (the moral law).
    (2)   Maxim A cannot be willed as universal
          law.
    (3)   Therefore, _____.

Clearly, the conclusion 'Do not act on A' follows
from (1) and (2).

B.

    (1)   Act only on a maxim that you can will
          to be universal law.
    (2)   _____.
    (3)   Therefore, do not act on A.

In this second instance, 'Maxim A cannot be willed
as a universal law' may be inferred from (1) and
(3). Or, rather, we would know that this is the
premise which must be supplied in order to make
the argument valid. In neither of these two cases
can any inference be made from the categorical imperative alone. Nor, furthermore, does the moral
law itself enable us to decide whether a particular
maxim can be universalized. The categorical imperative is decidedly not a test for maxims in the
sense of telling us whether certain maxims have
the characteristic of universalizability (whatever exactly this is) - this is a determination
which has to be made independently. The categorical imperative, then, is a normative principle
telling us what characteristics a maxim ought to
have, not what characteristics it does have. Kant
says as much as this in speaking of the 'type' of
the moral law:

> . . . in cases where the causality
> of freedom is to be judged, natural
> law serves only as a *type* of a law
> of freedom, for if common sense did
> not have something to use in actual
> experience as an example, it could
> make no use of the law of pure prac-
> tical reason in applying it to that
> experience.[82]

53

I understand Kant here to be saying that the categorical imperative by itself does not tell us whether a particular maxim can be universalized. This is why we need the 'type' of the moral law, to be able to apply the moral law to particular circumstances.

The question that is really at issue in discussing the universalizability, or the lack thereof, of particular maxims is the problem of Kant's moral epistemology. There is good reason to be concerned about this question since, as we have seen, Kant's views on the matter are far from clear. We have noted, however, that Kant seems to take the entire issue of moral epistemology as being of less significance than the normative grounding of his moral theory.[83] That is to say, Kant apparently thought that, once one has been persuaded that one ought to follow the categorical imperative, there is no great difficulty in discerning what sorts of maxims are consistent with that law. Kant may have been mistaken in thinking that the problems of moral epistemology are relatively simple, but there can be little doubt that this is his view.

If we grant for the moment that, once the moral law is selected as the determining ground for maxims, morally appropriate maxims follow for the most part, we should pause to see what this point tells us about the nature of Kant's moral theory. This seems to indicate that Kant is not primarily concerned with the business of presenting a procedure for deciding whether or not a particular maxim is morally suitable. On the subject of the need for a metaphysics of morals, Kant writes,

> A metaphysics of morals is therefore indispensable, not merely because of motives to speculate on the source of the a priori practical principles which lie in our reason, but also because morals themselves remain subject to all

kinds of corruption so long as
the guide and supreme norm for
their correct estimation is
lacking.[84]

On the issue of the relative need for a critique
of pure as opposed to practical reason, Kant
says, ". . . a critical examination of pure
practical reason is not of such extreme importance as that of speculative reason, because
human reason, even in the commonest mind, can
easily be brought to a high degree of correct-
ness and completeness in moral matters,"[85]
Are these two passages consistent? I think that
they are. Kant seems to be saying that, so long
as we do not understand the nature of the principles that underlie our morality, we are prone
to making mistakes, through the pursuit of
pleasure, or whatever. When he says that we
can easily be brought to a high degree of cor-
rectness, I think that he means that, once we
adopt the proper starting-point - the moral law -
we experience relatively little difficulty in
determining what morality requires of us.

I shall not dwell further here on the subject of Kant's moral epistemology, or upon the
related question whether Kant's moral theory
can in any meaningful sense be action-guiding.
The relation between these questions is clear:
if one cannot know whether one's proposed maxim
meets the standards of the moral law, one cannot
be guided by the moral law in deciding whether
to adopt the maxim. Readers interested in these
issues might wish, again, to consult Onora Nell's
Acting on Principle.[86] My primary interest here
is in the normative character of Kant's moral
theory, and with the logical distinctions he finds
it necessary to make in support of his normative
position. I therefore leave the discussion of
Kant's moral epistemology.

E. Some Problems with the Concept of the Human
   Willkür.

I shall now turn to a discussion of some

problems related to the human will. Among the topics to be discussed here are the following: (1) are there, within the human will, two faculties of choice, one phenomenal and one noumenal, or only one faculty of choice, with both phenomenal and noumenal aspects; (2) what are the consequences for Kant's position of the alternative responses to (1); (3) the distinctions between the moral law and the principle of self-love as the determining principles of the will, between freedom and heteronomy, and the relation of these distinctions to (1) and (2).

1.   How Many Willkür's?

There are difficulties that seem to rule out the two-Willkür interpretation: (1) the fact that Kant describes the human faculty of choice as *arbitrium liberum* would appear to rule out the possibility of its being either wholly phenomenal or wholly noumenal. If the human faculty of choice were wholly noumenal, the term *liberum* would not apply to it, and, furthermore, Kant terms the faculty of choice of a human being to be an *arbitrium sensitivum*, indicating it is susceptible to pathological influence. The term *liberum* would also not apply to a wholly phenomenal faculty of choice, as such a Willkür would not have the independence from determination by inclination that the term *liberum* connotes. It is important to note, once again, Kant's remarks regarding the character of the human will in the first Critique:

> . . . a will is sensuous, in so far
> as it can be pathologically affected,
> i.e., by sensuous motives; it is
> *animal (arbitrium brutum)* if it can
> be pathologically *necessitated*.
> The human will is certainly an
> *arbitrium sensitivum*, not, however,
> *brutum* but *liberum*. For sensibility
> does not necessitate its action.[87]

From this passage, it is quite clear that, while

Kant does think of the human will as sensuous, he does not consider it to be wholly sensuous, nor does he consider it to be wholly noumenal; (2) if there were two separate faculties of choice, there might be a far more formidable difficulty than merely that of relating the two to each other. That is, the faculty of choice of a holy will, if it has one at all, has, I have argued, no alternative as a supreme determining principle of its maxims other than the moral law. If the human will had one faculty of choice that was purely phenomenal and another that was purely noumenal, then that faculty of choice that was purely noumenal would be able to select only the moral law as its determining principle, while the purely phenomenal faculty of choice, presumably, would be an *arbitrium brutum* and would have to have the satisfaction of desire as its sole determining principle. That is, since the moral law is itself intelligible, or noumenal, then this would seem to eliminate it as a possible supreme determining principle of a purely phenomenal faculty of choice.[88] That is, a purely phenomenal faculty of choice would be one that could be considered only as appearance, and never as intelligence. Some of these remarks will become clearer when I discuss the 'causality' of the will later.

This discussion leads rather naturally into a discussion of Kant's analysis of the possibility of freedom in the Third Antinomy of the first Critique and of Kant's views of the 'causality' of the will. Although I am loath to enter upon a treatment of this thorny part of Kant's writings, it seems to be essential at this juncture.

NOTES - Chapter One

[1]Cf., Kant, _Critique I_, pp. A534, B562.

[2]Cf., _FMM_, pp. 445-6.

[3]Kant, _Metaphysical Elements of Justice_ (Ladd translation), p. 226. Henceforth, this work will be referred to as _Justice_. Pagination is from the Akademie edition.

[4]_Ibid._, p. 213.

[5]Cf., _FMM_, p. 440.

[6]Lewis White Beck, _Op.cit._, p. 131.

[7]Cf., _FMM_, p. 412; Kant, _Critique of Practical Reason_, (Beck translation), p. 5. Henceforth, this work will be referred to as the second _Critique_ in the text and as _Critique II_ in notes. All pagination is from the Akademie edition; Kant, _Justice_, p. 226: "The Will, which relates to nothing but the law . . . (and is therefore practical reason itself.)"

[8]_FMM_, p. 396.

[9]_Ibid._, p. 395.

[10]_Ibid._.

[11]_Ibid._, p. 396.

[12]_Ibid._, p. 412.

[13]_Ibid._, pp. 412-13.

[14]_Ibid._, p. 396.

[15]Lewis White Beck, _Op.cit._, p. 41.

[16]David Hume, _A Treatise of Human Nature_ (Selby-Bigge edition), Bk. II, Section III, p. 413.

[17]Ibid., pp. 414-15.

[18]Critique I, pp. A471, B499.

[19]Ibid., pp. A550, B578.

[20]Ibid., pp. A633, B661.

[21]FMM, p. 396.

[22]Cf., Critique I, pp. A106, Bxvii. In the first Critique, necessity is applied to phenomena, through the categories; in the moral philosophy, necessity applies to actions. Necessity applied to phenomena is, in Latin, *Necessitas*; necessity applied to actions is *Necessitatio*.

[23]FMM, p. 421.

[24]Kant, Lectures on Ethics, p. 15.

[25]John R. Silber, "The Ethical Significance of Kant's Religion," in the translator's introduction to Kant's Religion Within the Limits of Reason Alone, p. xciii.

[26]FMM, p. 414.

[27]Ibid., pp. 413-14.

[28]Ibid., p. 413.

[29]Ibid., p. 416.

[30]Ibid., p. 434.

[31]Ibid., p. 414.

[32]Cf., Ibid., p. 414. It seems that we must conceive of the holy will as having a faculty of choice if we are to think of it as acting at all. The holy will's perfection lies, as I have said, in its being able to choose only that which is in accordance with the moral law. This may seem to

some a peculiar conception of perfection. The notion of the perfection of a being, one might think, carries with it the idea of possessing something which imperfect beings do not possess, or of possessing something to a degree to which imperfect beings do not. To be sure, the holy will does possess the quality of being able to choose only that which is in accord with the moral law, and this is a quality that finite rational beings do not have. The reason, however, that a holy will lacks something which the will of a finite rational being does have - namely, the quality of being affected by sensuous inclinations, of being a part of the phenomenal world and, thereby, being able to choose things other than those in accord with the moral law. Without trying to trace the history of the concept of moral perfection, we may put our finger on the idea behind the point Kant is making: moral perfection consists in being incapable of doing anything wrong. God's perfection lies, along with other things, in the inability to be immoral.

[33]Critique I, pp. A534, B562.

[34]Ibid.

[35]Aristotle, Metaphysics, Bk XII, Ch. 7.

[36]Ibid.

[37]FMM, p. 414.

[38]Justice, p. 226.

[39]Leibniz, Selections (Wiener edition), p. 238.

[40]Cf., Aristotle, Metaphysics, Bk. I.

[41]Aristotle, Nicomachean Ethics (Ross translation), Bk. III, Ch. 2.

[42]Ibid., Ch. 3.

[43]Ibid.

[44]Ibid., my emphasis.

[45]Justice, p. 213.

[46]Aristotle, Nicomachean Ethics, Bk. III, Ch. 3.

[47]Ibid., Bk. II, Ch. 1.

[48]Ibid.

[49]FMM, p. 413.

[50]Aristotle, Nicomachean Ethics, Bk. II, Ch. 4.

[51]Ibid.

[52]FMM, pp. 412-13.

[53]Ibid., p. 397.

[54]Ibid.

[55]Aristotle, Nicomachean Ethics, Bk. II, Ch. 5.

[56]To say that the faculty of choice takes the moral law as the determining ground of its maxims means that it decides what maxims to act upon on the basis of what the moral law requires, rather than on the basis of what will serve other purpose (inclination) that one may happen to have.

[57]In discussing the transcendental unity of apperception, Kant makes it clear that he does not wish to 'reify' the distinction between the empirical and the non-empirical (transcendental) ego. He writes, "The synthetic unity of consciousness is, therefore, an objective condition of all knowledge. It is not merely a condition that I myself require in knowing an object, but is a condition under which every intuition must stand in order *to become an object for me*." (Critique I, p. B138) There is a distinction between one thing's being a necessary condition of something else, and the

former entity's having an existence apart from
that for which it is a condition. Of the limi-
tations on our knowledge of things, Kant writes,
"Our knowledge of the existence of things
reaches, then, only so far as perception and
its advance according to empirical laws can extend." (Ibid., pp. A226, B273-4). But this
limits our knowledge of existence to that which
can be given in sensible intuition and, of the
transcendental unity of apperception, Kant says,
"This *representation* is a *thought*, not an *intuition*." (Ibid., p. B157) The entire argument
of that section of the Transcendental Dialectic
known as the 'Paralogisms' is designed to show
that one can know nothing of the existence of a
non-empirical self. As Kant says, the ". . .
'I think' is the vehicle of all concepts, and
therefore also of transcendental concepts, . . .
and is itself transcendental. But it can have
no special designation, because it serves only
to introduce all our thought, as belonging to
consciousness." (Ibid., pp. A341, B399-400).
And, finally, "Through this I or he or it (the
thing) which thinks, nothing further is repre-
sented than a transcendental subject of the
thoughts = x. It is known only through the
thoughts which are its predicates, and of it,
apart from them, we cannot have any concept whatever." (Ibid., pp. A346, B404).

[58]Cf., Aristotle, Nicomachean Ethics, Bk. III,
Ch. 2, 3; Kant, Justice, p. 213.

[59]Lewis White Beck, Studies in the Philosophy of Kant, p. 227.

[60]FMM, p. 434.

[61]Jean-Paul Sartre, "Existentialism," in
Existentialism and Human Emotions, p. 15, my
emphasis.

[62]Aristotle, Nicomachean Ethics, Bk. II,
Ch. 4.

[63] Ibid.

[64] FMM, pp. 399-400.

[65] Ibid., p. 391.

[66] Cf., R. M. Hare, The Language of Morals, Ch. 4.

[67] FMM, p. 421fn.

[68] Ibid., p. 422, my emphasis.

[69] Ibid., pp. 406-07.

[70] Cf., Onora Nell, Acting on Principle, Ch. 2, 3.

[71] Ibid.

[72] Cf., Marcus G. Singer, Generalization in Ethics.

[73] Onora Nell, Op.cit., p. 12.

[74] Marcus G. Singer, Op.cit., p. 140.

[75] Ibid., p. 21.

[76] I have discussed this problem in more detail in my "The Generalization Argument Re-Visited," written with R. R. Brockhaus, Philosophical Studies, 1975.

[77] Cf., Onora Nell, Op.cit., pp. 28-9; David Lyons, Forms and Limits of Utilitarianism.

[78] Cf., Onora Nell, Op.cit., p. 42.

[79] FMM, p. 421fn.

[80] Ibid., p. 397.

[81] Lewis White Beck, translator's introduction to FMM, p. xvi.

[82] _Critique II_, p. 70.

[83] _FMM_, p. 391.

[84] _Ibid._, pp. 389-90.

[85] _Ibid._, p. 391.

[86] Onora Nell, _Op.cit_.

[87] _Critique I_, pp. A534, B562.

[88] This is, strictly speaking, a metaphysical consideration, but one which has rather obvious consequences for moral philosophy.

Chapter II

KANT'S THEORIES OF THE 'CAUSALITY' OF THE WILL

Introduction.

The third section of Kant's <u>Grundlegung</u> opens with the following passage:

> As will is a kind of causality
> of living beings so far as they
> are rational, freedom would be
> that property of this causality
> by which it can be effective in-
> dependently of foreign causes
> determining it . . .[1]

What, we may well wonder, does Kant mean in terming the will a 'causality'? The answer to this
question is far from being simple. Indeed, as I
shall show, there are three ways of conceiving of
the will as a 'causality'. This is owing to the
fact that Kant distinguishes between two senses
of 'will', <u>Wille</u> (the legislative will), and
<u>Willkür</u> (the faculty of choice). There is a sense
of the 'causality' of the will appropriate to each
of the senses of 'will', and a third sense of
'causality' applicable to the combined faculty.
There are also several senses or aspects of 'freedom', appropriate to the different senses of
'will'. The purpose of the present chapter is to
clarify the different senses of the 'causality' of
the will. Doing this will require analyzing a
range of other topics in Kant's philosophy, including: (1) the concepts of 'freedom' in the
first and second <u>Critiques</u>[2] and in <u>Religion Within
the Limits of Reason Alone</u>[3]; (2) the distinction
drawn by Kant between 'cause' and 'causality' in
the first <u>Critique</u>; (3) the relation of Aristotle's
doctrine of 'four causes' to Kant's theories. This
last point is of special significance, as I find
Aristotle's analysis of causation extremely

illuminating in this connection. It is not
clear to what extent, if any, Kant actually
read Aristotle, although there are occasional
references to 'Aristotelian principles' in
Kant's writings.[4] The significant point is
that Aristotle's views are philosophically re-
vealing, and I shall treat them in this light
without making any particular historical claims
about the relations between the two philosophers.

The chapter will be divided into the
following sections: (1) Aristotle's Doctrine
of 'Four Causes'; (2) The 'Causality' of Willkür;
(3) The 'Causality' of Wille; (4) The 'Causality'
of the Combined Faculty; (5) Concluding Remarks.
All of what has been said in Chapter I regarding
the Wille/Willkür distinction applies here.

A.   Aristotle's Doctrine of 'Four Causes'.

Kant is commonly taken as reacting to certain lines of argument in the empiricist tradition, and thus the suggestion that one ought
to think of Kant in relation to Aristotle may
seem strange to some. Nonetheless, I think that
many aspects of Kant's theory of the 'causality'
of the will may be illuminated by reference to
the doctrine of 'four causes' in Aristotle. In
this brief section, I want only to sketch the
four causes, and to prepare the way for later
analyses of the 'causality' of the will.

Of the doctrine of 'four causes' in general,
Ross has written, ". . . for Aristotle none of the
four causes is sufficient to produce an event;
. . . We have, then, to think of his 'causes' as
conditions necessary but not separately sufficient
to account for the existence of a thing;"[5]

The four causes themselves are, of course,
material, efficient, formal, and final causes. To
illustrate the distinctions between the causes, it
may be best to take a concrete example. Consider
the building of a house: the material cause will
be the lumber, nails, etc., that are used by the

laborer; the efficient cause will be the laborer
him/herself; the formal cause will be the conception of the finished dwelling in the mind of
the laborer (or, perhaps, the architect); the
final cause will be the end or purpose for the
sake of which the house is built, and here we
seem to have a choice as to what to cite as a
cause: it might be the satisfaction of the desire to keep a family safe and warm (this might
particularly be the case if the workers are
building the house for their own family) or it
might be to satisfy a desire to earn some money
by plying the carpenter's trade, or something
else, depending upon what the goal of the laborer
is.

As we move on to consider Kant's theories of
the 'causality' of the will, we shall see how important Aristotle's distinctions are to a proper
understanding of what Kant is doing. The sufficient causal account of an action, for Aristotle, must include all of the four 'modes' of
causality, and I think that the same is true for
Kant. We should proceed now to see which modes
of causality can properly be attributed to Kant's
senses of 'will'.

B.   The 'Causality' of Willkür

The human faculty of choice cannot, for Kant,
be understood as embodying all four of Aristotle's
modes of causality. Rather, I think it is the
case that we must view Willkür as an efficient
cause of actions, and of maxims of action. In this
section, I shall show how it is possible to think
of the faculty of choice in this vein, why the
faculty of choice cannot be regarded as embodying
other modes of causality as well, and, perhaps most
importantly for Kant's moral theory, how the faculty of choice can be viewed as a spontaneous
efficient cause.

1.   The Third Antinomy and the 'Causality' of
Willkür

To understand Kant's conception of the faculty

67

of choice as a 'causality', we must also com-
prehend his position regarding the possibility
of freedom, for Kant says, "We have finally re-
duced the definite concept of morality to the
idea of freedom."[6]   Kant's argument for the
possibility of freedom is presented, of course,
in the Third Antinomy of the first Critique.
Thus, this is a crucial section for the present
inquiry.   Commentators do not agree as to what
Kant's position is, and much of what I say here
is at odds with a good bit of the standard
commentary.

     The absolutely essential key to understand-
ing Kant's resolution of the Third Antinomy between freedom and natural necessity lies in the
recognition of his distinction between appearances and things-in-themselves.   The position
Kant wants to adopt here has, at first glance,
the look of wanting to have one's philosophical
cake and eat it, too:

>   That all events in the sensible
> world stand in thoroughgoing con-
> nection in accordance with un-
> changeable laws of nature is an
> established principle of the Trans-
> cendental Analytic, and allows of
> no exception.   The question,
> therefore, can only be whether
> freedom is completely excluded by
> this inviolable rule, or whether
> an effect, notwithstanding its
> being thus determined in accord-
> ance with nature, may not at the
> same time be grounded in freedom.[7]

It is important to be clear here about exactly
what it is that Kant wants to argue.   One might,
of course, assert that some events are expli-
cable by reference to laws of nature while others
are not, and that freedom must be assumed to
account for those events for which natural necessity is insufficient.   Kant's view, however, is
that there is a sense in which natural necessity

68

is sufficient to account for all events. He wants to argue, therefore, that, though all events are determinable by reference to laws of nature, freedom nevertheless has some role to play. The question, obviously, is what role freedom could have to play, given what appears to be a very strong claim for natural law that Kant makes here. The solution to this apparent dilemma lies in seeing just what it is that Kant means when he says that all events are 'determinable' by reference to laws of nature. I think it is the case that what he means is not so strong as it might seem. This is the point at which the distinction between appearances and things-in-themselves becomes so crucial. As Kant writes, ". . . if appearances are things-in-themselves, freedom cannot be upheld. Nature will then be the complete and sufficient determining cause of every event."[8]

Kant's distinction between appearances and things-in-themselves is so well-known that it probably requires little explication here. But why is the distinction so important for the possibility of freedom? Kant writes,

> If, on the other hand, appearances are not taken for more than they actually are; if they are viewed not as things in themselves, but merely as representations, connected according to empirical laws, they must themselves have grounds which are not appearances. The effects of such an intelligible cause appear, and accordingly can be determined through other appearances, but its causality is not so determined.[9]

Further, Kant concludes, "Thus, the effect may be regarded as free in respect of its intelligible cause, and at the same time in respect of appearances as resulting from them according to the necessity of nature."[10]

69

We should pause for a moment to make sure that we are also clear as to what Kant does not wish to argue. It can be shown that Kant does not intend to claim that all future events are, in principle, completely predictable. If this were the case, then freedom really would be impossible. Rather, what Kant wants to demonstrate is that, for any phenomenal event, it is in principle possible to trace backwards to antecedent phenomenal conditions which provide, as it were, a 'physical accounting' of the given event. Kant would not say that, given any set of phenomenal conditions, we can in principle predict exactly what will happen next (I keep employing the phrase 'in principle' here, because I want to emphasize that Kant's concern in defending natural necessity is to account for the possibility of engaging in scientific inquiry, and not to claim that science has actually succeeded in giving a coherent account of the world of sense). All of these points will become clear in the following analysis.

Does drawing the distinction between appearances and things-in-themselves really solve as much as Kant evidently thinks it does? We should note, first of all, that Kant is not developing his full theory of the freedom of the will here. Even if the analysis of the Antinomy stands scrutiny, more will be required to yield obligation to a categorical imperative. There is a distinctively normative dimension to Kant's theory of freedom which is not at issue at the present moment. But, we may suppose, there is even reason to wonder whether the resolution of the Antinomy itself can be maintained. Whatever else Kant's normative theory requires, it does need at least the theory of freedom for which Kant argues in the Third Antinomy. And, after all, what Kant is arguing here does sound very strange: appearances are one and all determinable by reference to laws of nature, and, nevertheless, these same appearances may, from a different standpoint, be regarded as the effects of an intelligible free causality - the will.

70

Kant anticipates this objection, and says,
". . . granting that effects are appearances and
that their cause is likewise appearance, is it
necessary that the causality of their cause
should be exclusively empirical?"[11] Having thus
posed so leading a question, Kant continues,

> May it not rather be, that while
> for every effect in the [field of]
> appearance a connection with its
> cause in accordance with the laws
> of empirical causality is indeed
> required, this empirical causality,
> without the least violation of its
> connection with natural causes, is
> itself an effect of a causality
> that is not empirical but intelli-
> gible?[12]

Several points are relevant to the discussion
here: Kant appears to want to draw a distinction
between the causal relations that obtain between
appearances within a series of appearances, and
the relation between the series as a whole and the
causality from which it originated. Given this
distinction, Kant can then argue that there is no
reason to deny the possibility of freedom as the
'originating' (efficient?) cause of a series of
appearances, even though it is in principle impossible to discover freedom as such a cause
within any given series. Indeed, it would be,
Kant could say, an instance of the 'fallacy of
composition' to suppose that a series of appearances as a whole must necessarily be caused in
the same way as the particular appearances within
the series; it now appears that Kant's thesis
about causality in accordance with laws of nature
is not, in fact, so strong as one might have supposed. Note Kant's words once again, "May it not
rather be, that while for every effect in the
[field of] appearance a connection with its cause
in accordance with the laws of empirical causality
is indeed required, this empirical causality,
without the least violation of its connection
with natural causes . . ."[13] It seems that Kant

is saying here that freedom can produce no effect which is contrary to the laws of nature, but not necessarily that physical laws in themselves produce every event.

There is further textual evidence that it is indeed Kant's view that, though all appearances are consistent with laws of nature, we cannot claim to know that all appearances are produced through laws of nature. A lengthy quotation will illustrate this point:

> If . . . I . . . arise from my
> chair, in complete freedom . . .
> a new series [of appearances]
> . . . has its absolute beginning
> in this event . . . For this reso-
> lution and act of mine do not form
> part of the succession of purely
> natural effects, and are not a
> mere continuation of them. In
> respect of its happening, natural
> causes exercise over it *no de-*
> *termining influence whatsoever.*
> It does indeed *follow upon them,*
> but *without arising out of them;*[14]

On the subject of being able to discover the phenomenal cause for any effect - the empirical condition within the series of appearances - Kant writes,

> If, however, what we are dealing
> with are appearances . . . I can-
> not say, in the same sense of the
> terms, that if the conditioned is
> given, all its conditions (as
> appearances) are likewise given,
> and therefore cannot in any way
> infer the absolute totality of
> the series of its conditions . . .
> What we can say is that a *regress*
> to the conditions, that is, a con-
> tinued empirical synthesis, on the

side of the conditions, is en-
joined or set as a task . . .[15]

This point is important to understanding Kant's
view regarding the strength of the causal link
between appearances. He seems to be saying that,
in principle, we can always search for causes
within the field of phenomena, not that we do,
in fact, always find causes within that field.
Also, I think that Kant must be interpreted as
saying that what we find when we do thus regress
upon empirical conditions are the conditions
from which the effect could have followed, or
by which the effect could have been produced,
and not that we find certain knowledge of antecedent causes. What we can be sure of is only
that present effects and past conditions will
always be compatible. Given the status, as
appearance, of the data with which physical science operates, this may be enough.

    Some will no doubt see this as a sub-
stantial weakening of the sort of claims physical science makes. I do not think this is the
case, although there is certainly room for dis-
pute on this. Science traditionally claims to
generate hypotheses about the way the world works,
and proceeds to generate data in support of
these hypotheses. No claim is to be made, or
at least none could be justified, for absolute
certainty as to the truth of these hypotheses.
I think that there may be room for real doubt
as to whether Kant's resolution of the Third
Antinomy ultimately yields a distinction between Kant's views of natural necessity and
Hume's conception of causality as constant conjunction plus some sort of psychological disposition to think of the conjunction in terms
of necessity. This is an important problem, but,
unfortunately, it is one that lies beyond the
scope of the present inquiry.

    Because of the distinction between appear-
ances and things-in-themselves, Kant is able to

draw a further separation between 'cause' (*Ursache*) and 'causality' (*Kausalität*). When Kant speaks of the relation *among* phenomena, he uses the term 'cause', and this bears a strong resemblance to Aristotle's notion of 'material cause', rather than to the more dynamic notion of 'efficient cause'. We shall see more about this presently.

I have been urging the adoption of what one might term a 'weak interpretation' of Kant's views on physical determinism. We should note, however, a further remark made by Kant that would seem to pose a difficulty for such an analysis: on the subject of the regress to empirical conditions, he writes, " . . . *in this regress* there can be no lack of given conditions."[16] This passage may be taken as suggesting a stronger claim, namely that, for any appearance, there is a sufficient causal explanation within the series of appearances, although I do not see it as necessitating that we understand Kant as committed to the stronger claim.

There are, of course, commentators who take Kant to be making a very strong claim about the status of natural necessity. One such commentator is R. P. Wolff, in his recent book The Autonomy of Reason. The flavor of Wolff's analysis of Kant comes clear in the following passage:

> . . . we must at least insist on understanding how my *causally determined behavior* [my emphasis] can legitimately be construed as even a *possible* effect of my rational agency . . . when I pull the trigger of the gun in my hand and slay my enemy, the full majesty of the Critique of Pure Reason stands behind the claim that may behavior was determined by alien causes . . .[17]

I shall presently show that there is ample evidence for the claim that the 'full majesty' of the first Critique stands elsewhere. Specifically, I shall argue that what Kant is firmly committed to is the proposition that there are always antecedent material causes (*Ursachen*) among the field of phenomena. On the question of efficient causality (*Kausalität*), Kant's language is much more guarded, and he does not, so far as I can see, assert that the efficient cause of each event must be phenomenal.

One way of characterizing what Kant is doing is to view him as reacting against the trend in 17th and 18th century physics to see all causality as empirical efficient causality. I take Kant to be moving in the direction of a broader, more Aristotelian analysis of 'cause'.[18]

John R. Silber is another of the commentators who attribute a very strong view of natural causation to Kant.[19] Silber's position, as I understand it, is that Kant's analysis of the Third Antinomy cannot resolve the problem of the conflict between freedom and natural necessity, and Kant gets himself out of the Antinomy only in the Critique of Judgment, and then only by rejecting the strong claims for natural causation, and opting for freedom. At one time, I agreed with the first part of Silber's claim (that Kant took a 'hard line' on natural necessity in the first Critique), and disagreed with the second (that the third Critique position represents a revision of Kant's first Critique views on natural necessity). I now disagree with both parts of Silber's claim, and think that Kant's Third Antinomy position on natural necessity is not so strong as Silber maintains.[20]

Lewis White Beck's views on the strength of Kant's claims for natural necessity and of the difficulties they cause for Kant's position are, I think, more formidable than those I have examined thus far. I shall therefore spend more time in

dealing with them. Beck takes Kant to be making
quite a strong claim for natural necessity and
says, "How can we hold a man responsible for his
actions and yet say, at the same time, that 'before ever they had happened, they are one and all
predetermined in the empirical character'?"[21]
I think that this passage may be accommodated
without necessarily committing Kant to the strong
view of natural necessity. I believe that the
passage from Kant's first Critique contained in
the quotation from Beck is badly translated.
The original German text reads:

> Jede derselben [referring to
> actions of the will] ist *im*
> *empirischen Charakter des*
> *Menschen* vorher bestimmt . . .[22]

A better translation of this would be, ". . .
they are one and all predetermined in the empirical character *of the person*." The significance
of adding the phrase 'of the person' is, potentially, two-fold: (1) the phrase could refer to
an individual person, and the actions of which he
or she is physically capable; or (2) to the notion
of a person in general, and the sorts of things
of which persons are physically capable. Either
way, the phrase suggests an analysis of Kant's
remarks which need not imply a 'hard line' interpretation of natural necessity.

Beck cites passages from the second Critique
that are more troublesome. I will quote directly
from Kant:

> It may be admitted that if it
> were possible for us to have so
> deep an insight into a man's
> character as shown both in inner
> and in outer actions, that every,
> even the least, incentive to
> these actions and all external
> occasions which affect them were
> so known us that his future con-
> duct could be predicted with as

76

great a certainty as the occurrences of a solar or lunar
eclipse, we could nevertheless
assert that the man is free.[23]

Beck reads this passage as committing Kant to a
strong view of natural necessity, which then
raises problems for the possibility of freedom.
Kant goes on to say,

. . . if we were capable of an
intellectual intuition of the
same subject, we would then discover that the entire chain of
appearances *with reference* to
that which *concerns only the
moral law*, depends upon the spontaneity of the subject as a
thing-in-itself, for the determination of which no physical explanation can be given.[24]

The crucial question that must be asked here
is: what *is* the status of our 'certainty' regarding such natural events as those mentioned in the
first of the two preceding quotations? Kant's
own words refer us back to the first Critique:
" . . . in order to remove the apparent contradiction between the mechanism of nature and freedom . . . we must remember what was said in the
Critique of Pure Reason."[25] Thus, we ought not
to let Kant's language in the second Critique
guide our understanding of the first Critique
doctrines; rather, any such guidance should run
in the other direction.

We have already seen much of what Kant says
about natural necessity in the Third Antinomy,
and we shall presently see more. Perhaps we
ought also to look at the Second Analogy, another
section in which Kant lays out his views on
natural causation. Here again, I think there
are grounds for adopting the sort of weaker interpretation of Kant's views on natural necessity
that I have been urging.

In the Second Analogy, Kant writes,

> . . . in the perception of an
> event there is always a rule
> that makes the order in which
> the perceptions [in the appre-
> hension of this appearance]
> follow upon one another a
> *necessary* order.[26]

What is Kant committed to by this passage? He
seems to be saying that, in order for my arm to
be raised from a position at my side to a position
perpendicular to my body, it must pass through a
position at an angle of 45°. My arm cannot appear
first at 60°, then at 45°, and then at 90°, it
necessarily passes through 45° first. It does
not say that my arm had to reach 90° in the first
place, since I might have stopped it sooner.

Consider another passage:

> If, then, we experience something
> that happens, we in so doing al-
> ways presuppose that something
> precedes it, on which it follows
> according to a rule.[27]

The key phrase in the original German text of this
passage is '*worauf* es nach einer Regel *folgt*'.
Compare this with the following passage from the
Third Antinomy: "It [the act of my arising from
my chair] does indeed *follow upon them* [natural
causes], but without *arising out of them*."[28]
Here, the German reads, ' . . . *auf* jene *folgt,*
aber *daraus* nicht *erfolgt*.'

There is a crucial difference between '*auf*
etwas *folgen*', and '*aus* etwas *erfolgen*'. The
former means 'follow upon in succession', whereas the latter signifies 'arise out of' or 'result from'. Clearly, an event might both 'follow
upon' and 'arise out of' the state of affairs preceding it. But Kant's language suggests that his
view is: (1) that an event need not do both, so

far as natural causes are concerned; (2) that an
event might 'follow upon' natural causes while at
the same time 'arising out of' free efficient
causality. Kant's language is quite consistent
between the Second Analogy and the Third Antinomy,
and I suggest that it supports my analysis.[29]

Perhaps Kant does wish to make this stronger
claim after all but, if he does, it seems to me
that it will cause real problems for his assertion that free causality is possible. For
example, suppose we take an hypothetical event
of Jones shooting Smith. If we ask what caused
the death of Smith, we could proceed directly to
the bullet through the heart, and then backtrack
to the weapon and, sooner or later, arrive at
Jones. But, there seems to be no particular
reason to stop at the moment when Jones enters
the picture. We can ask why Jones shot Smith,
and, presumably, get an answer in terms of causal
relations among phenomena. At least, there would
always be an answer in principle--whether we can
always find the answer in practice, or agree on
the answer, is quite another question, and quite
irrelevant at the moment. We might find ourselves
led, along this path, to talk of Jones' childhood,
his parents' divorce (Jones did have a tough life
. . .), and what have you. Can we then still maintain that Jones freely chose to shoot Smith, and
that he is therefore morally culpable in the death
of Smith? Obviously, this is what we must be able
to prove if Kant's 'proof' of the possibility of
freedom is to be worth anything whatever. I do
not see how the strong claim regarding the causal
connections among all appearances can be maintained if freedom is to be saved. That is, I
think that Kant must be interpreted as saying
that any empirical event will necessarily be consistent with prior empirical conditions--nothing
whatever happens that is physically impossible--
but that we need not assume that the prior physical conditions themselves produced or were the
efficient cause behind a given effect. The effect
might have been the result of an intelligible
free cause.

Defenders of the stronger interpretation of Kant's claim about natural necessity may respond that, so long as the distinction between a series of appearances as a whole and occurrences within a series is maintained, the strong interpretation can be defended. That is, the series of appearances might be thought of as beginning with 'Jones pulling the trigger', and ending with 'Smith lying on the pavement'. Within the series, all segments are causally connected. Nevertheless, Jones freely chose to initiate the series. It seems arbitrary, though, to take the series as necessarily beginning with 'Jones pulling the trigger'. One can scarcely imagine a defense attorney trying to defend a client this way. Thus I see no way, compatible with the possibility of freedom, of defending a strong interpretation of Kant's claims about the relations among appearances, and I therefore opt for the weaker, but I think, more sound, interpretation.

I think that what I have here termed the 'weak interpretation' of Kant's analysis of the Third Antinomy shows clearly why the distinction between things-in-themselves and appearances is of such great significance. If there were no such distinction, then our choices would be part of the world of sense, and determined by its laws. The crucial distinction between an event's being compatible with antecedent conditions and its being determined by antecedent conditions would cease to be a real distinction.

2.   Willkür as Spontaneous Efficient Cause.

Having seen Kant's position regarding the possibility of freedom, we should now proceed to examine what this tells us about the 'causality' of the faculty of choice. The distinction already noted between 'cause' (*Ursache*) and 'causality' (*Kausalität*) is important here. Kant argues for the possibility of transcendental freedom as a necessary condition of practical freedom. He says,

> . . . practical freedom pre-
> supposes that although some-
> thing has not happened, it
> *ought* to have happened, and
> that its cause [as found] in
> the [field of] appearance, is
> not, therefore, so determining
> that it excludes a causality of
> our will . . .[30]

The concept of a 'cause' (*Ursache*) seems to be
closest to Aristotle's notion of a material cause.
It is the 'stuff' of which actions are made. That
is, in order for me to arise from a chair, I must
first be sitting in one. All particular actions
are like this, in that certain concrete material
circumstances are required for their performance.
The concept of a 'causality' (*Kausalität*), on
the other hand, is like Aristotle's concept of an
efficient cause, or the 'moving force' behind an
action. What Kant appears to be saying in the
resolution of the Third Antinomy, then, is that
the material cause for an action may lie within
the field of appearance, while the efficient cause
is free and lies beyond that field. The Willkür
can thus be conceived as an efficient cause of
appearances.

When the faculty of choice is thus conceived
as an efficient cause, it is a spontaneous efficient cause. As Kant writes, "By freedom . . . in
its cosmological meaning, I understand the power
of beginning a state *spontaneously*."[31] That is,
when the faculty of choice causes an action, it
does so without being completely determined to do
so by antecedent conditions.

We must be careful here to distinguish between the notions of spontaneity and autonomy.
Spontaneity is, as I understand it, a metaphysical
concept, while the notion of autonomy (the property of the will to be a 'law to itself') is
normative. G. E. Moore argues that Kant commits
the 'naturalistic fallacy' in grounding morality
on a metaphysical principle like transcendental

freedom.[32]   However, I do not think that this is
the case.   It is one thing to say that normative
theory has some conditions which are not themselves normative, and quite another to assert
that normative theory derives directly from non-
normative conditions.   Kant affirms the former
position, but not the latter.   R. M. Hare argues
that no normative (evaluative) conclusion can be
validly inferred from a set of premisses contain-
ing no normative statements whatever.[33]   Hare
does not say that no normative conclusion can be
validly inferred from a set of premisses contain-
ing any non-normative statements whatever.   This,
of course, would be ridiculous.   It would be
equally ludicrous for Kant to attempt to derive
his normative theory solely from what he says
about the freedom of Willkür in the first Critique,
but Kant knows this as well as any of us.

   The reason why it is important to distinguish
between spontaneity and autonomy is that failing
to do so would lead us to the conclusion that
all actions of the faculty of choice are autonomous, and this is absurd.   Rather, Kant's view is
that all free choices of the will are spontaneous,
for, if they were not, they could not be imputed
to us as either praiseworthy or blameworthy.[34]
Our choices are autonomous only when the will takes
its own legislation as the guide to its actions.
Autonomy is thus a sub-class of spontaneity.

   Since the faculty of choice must be conceived
as influenced by, but not determined by, pathological affectations, the Willkür is the efficient
cause of actions, even in those cases in which the
will is responding to the pull of inclination.
This is an important point, because it is possible
to take some of the things Kant says as meaning
that the will is an efficient cause only in those
cases in which it is acting autonomously.

3.   Willkür as Partial Material Cause.

   I think that we may also say that the faculty
of choice is, in a sense, a 'partial material

cause' of actions, or, at least, of the maxims of action. That is, the disposition of the will to choose in certain ways is part of the set of conditions which serves as the material cause of the arising of any particular maxim. One might term the disposition to act in certain ways part of the efficient cause of maxims, but I do not think this would be quite correct. The faculty of choice must elect its disposition and, in the case of any particular maxim, it must elect to act out of its disposition. In Religion, Kant writes,

> The disposition, *i.e.*, the ulti-
> mate subjective ground of the
> adoption of maxims, can be one
> only and applies universally to
> the whole use of freedom. Yet
> this disposition itself must
> have been adopted by free choice,
> for otherwise it could not be
> imputed.[35]

The disposition, once formed, seems to me to serve as a part of the background against which particular maxims are chosen, and thus the disposition is part of the material cause. But perhaps this is nit-picking. I am more concerned that it be clear that the sense of 'cause' which Kant primarily attributes to the Willkür in the Third Antinomy is the sense of efficient cause.

C.   The 'Causality' of Wille.

It should be clear from the preliminary remarks of the first section that, if the legislative faculty of the will is to be conceived as a 'causality' at all, it must be a different sense (or senses) of 'cause' than that appropriate to Willkür. Wille relates to legislation for the maxims of action, rather than to actions *per se*. It is also neither free nor unfree, according to Kant, and this would seem to provide at least *prima facie* grounds for attributing a different sense of 'cause' to Wille. Of the legislative faculty, Kant writes,

> Laws proceed from the Will
> [Wille]; maxims, from the
> will [Willkür]. In man, the
> will is free. The Will, which
> relates to nothing but the law,
> cannot be called either free or
> unfree, for it relates, not to
> actions, but immediately to legi-
> slation for the maxims of action
> . . .36

In what sense, then, can we possibly conceive of
the legislative faculty as a 'causality' at all?
To make sense of calling the legislative faculty
a 'causality', three questions must be answered:
(1) what are the effects of which Wille is the
cause; (2) in what sense of 'cause' does the legislative faculty determine its effects; (3) is
Wille a sufficient cause of its effects, or
only a partial cause?

1.   The Effects of Wille.

    Wille's effects are maxims or, more pre-
cisely, the Willkür's choosing of maxims. When
Kant speaks of reason as determining the will,37
I think we must understand this as meaning Wille,
the legislative faculty, determining the faculty
of choice. Thus the effects of which the Wille
is cause are the choices of Willkür, in those
instances in which the faculty of choice is determined by Wille. This last phrase, 'in those
instances . . .' is absolutely crucial here. As
we shall see, to suppose that the faculty of choice
is always determined in its actions by the legislative will would be to conflate the human will
with the holy will.

    Is there anything else of which Wille can be
said to be a 'cause'? I think we may say that
Wille is a partial cause, along with the particu-
lars of an individual's circumstances, of an
action's being objectively necessary, i.e.,

84

morally obligatory. Kant writes, ". . . if the
will is not of itself in complete accord with
reason, . . . then the actions which are recognized as objectively necessary are subjectively
contingent. . ."[38] The part of this passage
that is important at the moment is the reference
to actions which are 'objectively necessary'.
Were it not for Wille's legislation, no actions
whatever would be objectively necessary. The
reference in the preceding passage to actions
as 'subjectively contingent' will be discussed
in more detail presently.

2.   Wille as Formal and Final Cause.

        Having asserted that certain choices by
Willkür and the objective necessity of certain
actions are the effects of which the legislative
faculty is the cause, it remains to be explained
in what sense the legislative faculty is the
'cause' of these effects. It seems to me that
there are two senses in which Wille may be a
'cause', depending in part upon which of Wille's
effects is being considered. The legislative
faculty is, I think, the formal cause (in Aristotle's sense of this expression) of the objective necessity of actions. That is, Wille is the
legislator of the law which dictates the 'struc-
tural requirements' to which our volitions ought
to conform. All actions ought to be such that
their maxims can be willed as universal law.
Kant is quite clear in thinking of this as a
formal requirement, as he writes, ". . . an act
from duty wholly excludes the influence of inclination and therewith every object of the will."[39]
If all objects of the will are excluded, there remain only formal characteristics to determine the
will.

        In instances in which the faculty of choice
acts from duty, I think that we may also say that
the Wille provides a law which is then the final
cause of Willkür's choosing. By 'final cause',
of course, I mean that the moral law is that for

85

the sake of which Willkür chooses.

It is tempting to think of the legislative faculty as being also an efficient cause, a moving force behind Willkür's choices. Kant does speak repeatedly of duty as behind a motive or incentive for the will, and such remarks have the impact of inclining us to think of the legislative faculty as an efficient cause. But, I think this would be a mistake in the final analysis, for several reasons: (1) it seems that Wille does not act but is, rather, an 'unmoved mover'[40]. It is difficult to see how anything could be an efficient cause without itself moving; (2) the terms Kant uses most frequently in connection with the notion of Wille as motive are *Bewegungsgrund* and *Bewegungsursache*, and neither of these really connotes any moving force on the part of the legislative faculty itself, but, rather, suggest that it is that to which the faculty of choice is drawn, or to which the faculty of choice draws itself; (3) Kant's theory of the freedom of the faculty of choice ultimately precludes the possibility of Wille's being an efficient cause of choice. Indeed, I think it is the case that nothing whatever, other than the faculty of choice itself, can be an efficient cause of its actions.

This last point is worthy of elaboration. Of the faculty of choice, Kant writes, "Man *himself* must make or have made himself into whatever, in a moral sense, whether good or evil, he is or is to become. Either condition must be an effect of his free choice [Willkür]."[41] Thus it is Kant's view that nothing determines the faculty of choice efficiently unless it chooses to be so determined. As John Silber writes,

> The human Willkür is influenced
> but not wholly determined by im-
> pulses: its actions are always
> determined according to the strong-
> est impulse, but only after the
> Willkür itself has made the

> decision by which the strongest
> impulse is determined . . . No
> impulse or desire can be a de-
> termining incentive for the
> Willkür until the Willkür
> chooses to make it so.[42]

Thus I think we must say that, for Kant, the
efficient cause of Willkür's choices must be considered to be the faculty of choice itself,
rather than anything outside of the faculty
of choice.

This last remark may seem to tread danger-
ously close to saying that moral action is
heteronomous, but this is not the case. When
Kant says that the moral worth of actions depends upon their being the results of autonomy,
he does not mean that the faculty of choice
does not go beyond itself in seeking a law to
guide its actions; rather, Kant says that
autonomy is a property of the will to be a law
to itself.[43] In this line from the Grundlegung,
Kant is not distinguishing between the two senses
of 'will' but is referring to the joint faculty,
encompassing both Wille and Willkür.

3.   Wille as Sufficient or Partial Cause.

Thus far, we have seen that Wille may be considered as, in different respects, both a formal
and a final cause of the actions of the faculty
of choice. It remains to be considered whether
the Wille can ever be a sufficient cause of
Willkür's choices. By now the answer should be
obvious: the legislative faculty cannot be a
sufficient cause of the actions of the faculty of
choice. To the extent that the various senses of
'cause' mean for Kant what they do for Aristotle,
it is clear that the sufficient conditions for
any event must include all four modes of causality:
material, efficient, formal, and final. To quote
David Ross once again, ". . . for Aristotle none
of the four causes is sufficient to produce an

87

event; . . . We have, then, to think of his 'causes' as conditions necessary but not separately sufficient to account for the existence of a thing."[44]

If it is clear that Wille can never be, by itself, the sufficient cause of the actions of the faculty of choice, it remains to inquire whether it is in fact a necessary condition of Willkür's actions. I think that it is, in two senses: (1) Wille's legislation is a necessary condition of the possibility of an action's having moral worth; (2) Wille's legislation is a necessary condition of Willkür's freedom as absolute spontaneity, in that the faculty of choice cannot be completely spontaneous unless it has alternatives for choice other than the service of one inclination or another. The first sense of necessity here refers to Wille as a final cause, the second to the legislative faculty as a formal cause.

The first sense in which Wille's legislation is a necessary condition of the actions of the faculty of choice is obvious, but the second requires some explanation. How could an absolute spontaneity be thought of as conditioned? The idea seems absurd on its face. But it is not at all absurd, and it is important to see why. The point is that the faculty of choice cannot be truly 'free', in the strongest sense of that term, if its only alternatives are choices among different inclinations. This is why the assumption, so frequently made by utilitarian moralists, that persons can be moved only by conceptions of pleasure and pain, renders morality in Kant's sense quite impossible.[45] The Wille's legislation provides the kind of 'radical alternative' necessary if the faculty of choice is to be truly 'free', i.e., independent of complete determination through inclination, or objects of desire. Only if there can be actions which are categorically required, rather than merely hypothetically required, can the will be truly independent of inclination. Wille's legislation is, as I have said, the formal condition under which actions can be categorically required.

There is an objection looming on the horizon, and it ought to be confronted and dispatched. It might be charged that, since the faculty of choice is really independent of Wille's legislation, the relation between the two senses of 'will' is really a contingent rather than necessary one. This view is wrong-headed. It is a contingent matter whether there is morality in Kant's sense at all, just as, I think, Kant views it as a contingent matter whether there is any knowledge whatever. That is, there is no necessity in our being bound by moral law: if we were creatures of a different sort, we might not be obligated categorically at all, just as lower animals are not obligated. But to think that Kant is trying to show that we are categorically bound to the moral law would be to misunderstand the nature of his project. Just as Kant takes it as obvious that we do have empirical knowledge, he also takes it as quite obvious that we have a sense of obligation. The question then becomes, as he writes, ". . . how are all these imperatives possible?"[46] And, then, "To see how the imperative of morality is possible is, then, without doubt the only question needing an answer."[47] It is in regard to the question of the possibility of a categorical imperative that the relation between Wille and Willkür is a necessary one.

There is yet another question which I will mention here, but which I will not discuss in detail until the concluding section. I have said that the legislative faculty is the formal cause of the objective necessity of actions. I think it is also, or can be, the formal cause of actions having moral worth. That is, when the faculty of choice chooses to follow the requirements of morality, the legislative faculty is both formal and final cause. But, when the actions of the faculty of choice are merely in accord with duty, Wille ceases to be either formal or final cause. I shall explain this in my concluding remarks.

D. The 'Causality' of the Joint Faculty of the
    Will.

It remains to combine our discussions of
the 'causality' of the separate aspects of the
will into a unified picture of the 'causality'
of the joint faculty of the will. I think it
may be argued that the joint faculty of the will
is the 'cause' of actions in three senses:
efficient, formal, and final. A certain kind of
dilemma admittedly appears to arise from this
assertion, namely that this would seem to render
the will in the final analysis insufficient to
account for the moral worth of actions. If this
should prove to be the case, it would be quite
damaging to Kant's position, but I think it can
be shown that Kant's view avoids the difficulty.
This problem, also, I will discuss in the concluding section.

The questions to be answered in this section
are essentially those raised when dealing with
the 'causality' of Willkür and Wille, respectively:
(1) what are the effects of which the combined
will is the cause; (2) in what sense(s) is the
combined will the 'cause' of its effects; (3)
is the combined faculty of the will a sufficient
cause or only a partial cause of its effects?

In order for us to consider the combined
faculty of the will to be considered as a 'causality' at all, it must be made clear that we are
considering actions done from duty, i.e., actions
having moral worth. This is the case, because it
is only such actions to which the legislative faculty of the will can be said to be causally related
in any sense. Actions which are done from a motive
other than duty will still have Willkür as an
efficient cause, but the formal and final causes
of such actions must be something other than the
legislative faculty. This seems to be equally true,
whether the action in question be in accord with
or opposed to duty. This last point bears on the
above-mentioned question of the legislative faculty

as formal and final cause, and will be dealt
with in the concluding section. It indicates
that, so far as <u>Wille</u>'s 'causality' in relation
to maxims is concerned, the formal and final elements cannot be separated off from one another.
That is, the formal and final aspects of <u>Wille</u>'s
'causality' are necessarily bound together, in
those instances in which <u>Wille</u>'s legislation is
a 'cause' at all.

From what has been said above, it seems to
follow that it is actions having moral worth of
which the combined faculty of the will is the
'cause'. Is this consistent with what Kant says
about the moral worth of actions? Recall Kant's
words:

> The good will is not good be-
> cause of what it effects or accom-
> plishes or because of its ade-
> quacy to achieve some proposed
> end; it is good only because of
> its willing, i.e., it is good of
> itself.[48]

And, further,

> An action performed from duty
> does not have its moral worth in
> the purpose which is to be
> achieved through it but in the
> maxim by which it is determined.
> Its moral value, therefore, does
> not depend on the realization of
> the object of the action but merely
> on the principle of volition by
> which the action is done, without
> any regard to the objects of the
> faculty of desire.[49]

I do not think that saying that morally worthy
actions are the effects of which the combined
faculty of the will is the 'cause' conflicts with
anything Kant says. While it is true that, for
Kant, the moral worth of actions does not depend

on the outcome, it does not follow that morally
worthy actions are not actions. Kant nowhere
says that actions having moral worth have no
outcome; he says only that their moral worth
does not depend on the outcome, but, rather, on
the maxim. It is the morally appropriate maxim
that is the effect of which the combined faculty
of the will is 'cause', but these maxims are,
after all, maxims of action.

The combined faculty of the will would appear
to be the 'cause' of moral acts in three senses:
efficient, formal, and final. The actual performance of any specific action also requires a
certain set of material circumstances which serve
as the material cause. Given that, in Aristotle's
sense of 'cause', all four modes of causality must
be present in order to produce a given event[50],
the combined faculty of the will seems not to be
sufficient to account fully for any particular
action. This observation, of course, raises the
difficulty mentioned at the outset of this section:
does Kant's theory of the 'causality' of the will
result in our having to say that the will is not
sufficient to produce morally worthy actions? We
shall come to this in the concluding section.

E.   Concluding Remarks.

There are several important problems to be
discussed in concluding these remarks on Kant's
theory of the 'causality' of the will. We need to
investigate why it is that the proper context within which to consider the 'causality' of the legislative faculty of the will is the class of actions
having moral worth rather than the class of actions
in general. Further, it is important to see the
sense in which the 'causality' of the will can be
said to be sufficient to produce actions of moral
worth. Before dealing with these issues, though,
it will be well to review briefly what we have
seen thus far.

The faculty of choice, owing to the absolute

spontaneity Kant attributes to it, must be considered to be the efficient cause of actions, whether these actions be of moral worth or not. The legislative faculty, in those instances when the Willkür elects to be determined by the moral law, is both formal and final cause of Willkür's choices, and hence, for the actions chosen. The combined faculty of the will appears to be efficient, formal, and final cause of actions having moral worth, although it does not seem to be the case that the combined faculty can be taken as sufficient in itself to produce actions having moral worth.

This last point, of course, is one of the problems arising out of this kind of analysis of Kant's position. Perhaps we can deal with it first. It would be disastrous for Kant's theory if it should turn out that the human will is insufficient to account for the moral worth of actions. Here we have to distinguish carefully between two similar but decisively different expressions: 'actions having moral worth' and 'the moral worth of actions'. I think that Kant's theory of the 'causality' of the will allows us to say that, while the will is insufficient to produce the former, it is quite sufficient for the latter. Furthermore, it is the latter that is *required* by Kant's conception of morality, and not the former.

The focus of the expression 'actions having moral worth' is action itself, while the focus of 'the moral worth of actions' is the feature moral worth which can be an attribute of actions under certain conditions. Clearly, it would be a fallacy to suppose that, because the will is insufficient to produce actions, that it is equally insufficient to produce some attribute of actions, namely moral worth.

The question that needs attention here is not the question of the will's sufficiency with regard to actions themselves, but that of the will's relation to that which is of moral worth within an action, namely the maxim. Here I think

93

the answer must be that the will is indeed sufficient to produce that which has moral worth within an action, i.e., its maxim.

But is the matter really so simple as this? How do maxims themselves arise? Kant is never clear about this point, and it should give us some pause. If we are to be true to an Aristotelian analysis of Kant's theory of the 'causality' of the will, we must say that all four modes of causality must be present to produce an action. Must it also be asserted that all four modes are required to produce a maxim of action? This matter is simply unclear in Kant, I think, but it seems that we can say one of two things: (1) that, while all of Aristotle's modes of causality are necessary to produce a maxim, the material aspect of a maxim is not relevant to the question of the maxim's moral worth. In this case, we can still say that the will is sufficient to produce that aspect of a maxim which has moral worth; (2) that the production of a maxim does not require a material cause. This latter interpretation is tempting, because, first of all, a maxim is a principle of action, and not an action, and, secondly, because it permits us to say, quite straightforwardly, that the will is sufficient to account for moral worth. Indeed, I think it is the case that the latter interpretation is the correct one, and seeing why is important to our inquiry.

The view David Ross attributes to Aristotle is that the four modes of causality are required to account for the existence of things.[51] There is an important sense in which, for Kant, actions are 'things', and an equally important sense in which maxims are not. Actions appear phenomenally, while maxims do not. We have to refer to maxims, and the choice of them, if we are to impute actions to persons at all, but these maxims are not themselves phenomenally given. It is, I think, only those 'things' which can appear phenomenally that can be said to require material causes in any strong sense of that notion. We should be clear, too, that the sense of 'material cause' that applies to Kant seems different from that which we find in Aristotle, in that, for Kant, the notion of 'material cause' will not refer to any 'stuff' underlying appearances.

If there is any sense at all in which maxims must have a material cause, it will be that our perception of the circumstances of our action may limit the range of options we take to be open to us, and this will in turn limit the range of maxims upon which we would be able to act. But this cannot be taken as 'causing' a particular maxim, and, even if it could, it is really our perception of the situation that is causally connected to the choice of maxim, and this is not something 'material' in any meaningful sense.

Thus I conclude that Kant's theory of the 'causality' of the will does account for the moral worth of actions, and that Kant's view therefore does not suffer from what would be otherwise a disastrous defect. It remains to discuss the other problem previously mentioned: why is the 'causality' of the legislative faculty, as formal and final cause of morally worthy actions, such that the two modes of causality cannot be separated? That is, why cannot the Wille be either the formal but not final, or final but not formal, cause of actions having moral worth? The answer to this lies in recalling that, for Kant, the moral worth of actions consists not only in the action's being in accordance with duty, but also in the action's being done for the sake of duty. When an action is done for the sake of duty or the moral law, then the legislative faculty of the will is the final cause of the action: Wille's legislation is that 'for the sake of which' the action is done. But, in such a case, the formal cause of the action will also be the moral law or, what seems to amount to the same thing for Kant, the conception of humanity as an end.[52] The notion of a 'formal cause' in general signifies the concept of the end to be realized

through the action. For Kant, the formal cause
of an action having moral worth must be the concept of treating humanity as an end in itself,
but this, as I have said, appears to mean the
same thing as saying that the action is done for
the sake of the moral law. Thus the formal and
final cause are the same in the case of actions
having moral worth.

What of the case in which the action in
question is done from a motive other than duty?
Might we not say that the action nonetheless has
the moral law as its formal cause, though it
clearly cannot have the law as its final cause?
I think the answer is no, but we need to see why.
Here, I am considering only actions which are in
accordance with duty, since Kant would certainly
consider actions opposed to duty to have something
other than Wille's legislation as either formal or
final cause. But what of an action in accordance
with duty, say, that of a merchant giving honest
service to an inexperienced customer. If the
merchant gives such service from the motive of
personal gain--e.g., maintaining a good reputation
in the community--obviously the act has the satisfaction of the personal motive as its final cause.
But why could we not say that the action nonetheless has the moral law as its formal cause, since
the action is in accordance with duty? I would
say that, though Kant sometimes uses the term
'maxim' in ambiguous ways, he would say that, in
the case in which the merchant gives honest service for personal gain, the concept of the end to
be achieved by the action would be different than
in the case where the merchant acted from duty.
In the former case, the merchant's objective is
his good standing in the community (or some such
thing), whereas in the latter case, the objective
is treating the customer as a person, period. Thus
the formal cause in the case in which the merchant
acts for personal gain is a conception of self-
interest, and the same self-interest is also the
motive, or final cause.

What have we learned, then, about Kant's

96

theories of the 'causality' of the will? If
nothing else, we have seen that the notion of
'causality' in this connection is far more com-
plicated than the few words Kant says about it
in the third section of the _Grundlegung_ would
lead us to suppose. Kant's distinction between
the two senses of 'will', _Wille_ and _Willkür_, is,
as noted, essential to understanding Kant's
various remarks about the 'causality' of the will,
as is also Aristotle's doctrine of 'four causes'.
In this latter connection, we have seen how an
analysis of Kant in terms of Aristotle's four
modes of causality enables us to grasp both
Kant's true position regarding the apparent conflict between freedom and natural necessity, and
also his views of the relation between actions,
maxims, and the moral law.

   Most of what I have said here is relevant
to what we might call the 'metaphysical' side of
Kant's analysis of the will and the moral law.
There is also a substantial normative side to the
question. That is, we may see, from what has
preceded these concluding remarks, what Kant
means when he calls the will a 'causality', and
how the two senses of 'will' relate to maxims, to
actions, and to each other. We have not seen much
about why the faculty of choice ought to elect the
moral law as the formal and final cause of maxims,
but this would be a story in itself, and quite a
long one at that. We shall proceed to this in the
remaining chapters.

NOTES - Chapter Two

[1]Kant, <u>Foundations of the Metaphysics of Morals</u> (Beck translation), pp. 445-6. Henceforth, this work will be referred to as <u>Grundlegung</u> in the text and as <u>FMM</u> in the notes. All pagination is from the Akademie edition.

[2]Kant, <u>Critique I</u>.

[3]Kant, <u>Religion Within the Limits of Reason Alone</u> (Greene & Hudson translation). Pagination from the Harper Torchbook edition. Further references to this work will be to <u>Religion</u>.

[4]Cf., Kant, <u>Metaphysical Principles of Virtue</u> (Ellington translation), pp. 404-5, 432, 433n., 470. Henceforth, this work will be referred to as <u>Virtue</u>. All pagination is from the Akademie edition.

[5]W. D. Ross, <u>Aristotle</u>, p. 73.

[6]<u>FMM</u>, p. 448.

[7]<u>Critique I</u>, pp. A536, B564.

[8]<u>Ibid</u>.

[9]<u>Ibid</u>., pp. A537, B565.

[10]<u>Ibid</u>.

[11]<u>Ibid</u>., pp. A544, B572.

[12]<u>Ibid</u>.

[13]<u>Ibid</u>.

[14]<u>Ibid</u>., pp. A451, B479.

[15]<u>Ibid</u>., pp. B527, A499.

[16]<u>Ibid</u>., p. A499.

[17]R. P. Wolff, The Autonomy of Reason, p. 204 (Harper Torchbooks, 1973).

[18]Cf., Thomas S. Kuhn, The Essential Tension, I, 2, pp. 21-30 (University of Chicago, 1977).

[19]Cf., John R. Silber, op.cit.

[20]For a more detailed look at my former position, see my "The Compatibility of Freedom and Natural Necessity in Kant" (Bucknell Review, Spring 1977).

[21]Lewis White Beck, A Commentary on Kant's Critique of Practical Reason, p. 191.

[22]Critique I, pp. A553, B581, my emphasis.

[23]Critique II, p. 99.

[24]Ibid., my emphasis.

[25]Ibid., p. 97.

[26]Critique I, pp. A193, B238.

[27]Critique I, pp. A195, B240.

[28]Critique I, pp. A451, B479, my emphasis.

[29]There was a recent debate in the journals between Lewis White Beck and Jeffrie Murphy on the question of the meaning of the Second Analogy and what it shows about Kant's position. See L. W. Beck, "Once More Unto the Breach: Kant's Answer to Hume, Again" (Ratio, vol. 9, no. 1, June, 1967; J. Murphy, "Kant's Second Analogy as an Answer to Hume" (Ratio, vol. 11, no. 1, June, 1969); L. W. Beck, "Rejoinder to Professors Murphy and Williams" (Ratio, vol. 11, no. 1, June 1969). The debate is reprinted in Philosophical Problems of Causation, ed. by Tom L. Beauchamp (Dickenson, 1974). I see nothing in any of these articles that would tend to refute my position.

[30]*Critique I*, pp. A534, B562.

[31]*Ibid*., pp. A533, B561.

[32]G. E. Moore, *Principia Ethica*, Ch. 4.

[33]R. M. Hare, *The Language of Morals*, Ch. 1,2.

[34]Cf., *Religion*, p. 20.

[35]*Ibid*.

[36]*Justice*, p. 226.

[37]*FMM*, p. 412.

[38]*Ibid*., pp. 412-3.

[39]*Ibid*., p. 400.

[40]In Aristotle's sense of this notion.

[41]*Religion*, p. 40.

[42]John R. Silber, *Op.cit*., p. cv.

[43]Cf., *FMM*, p. 440.

[44]W. D. Ross, *Op.cit*., p. 73.

[45]It would be a project in itself, and an interesting one at that, to examine a range of utilitarian writers to see the ways in which they deal with the question of human motivation. There is no space here to explore this issue in detail. For my present purposes, I will only cite a few selected passages to illustrate my contention that, for utilitarians, the claim that persons can be motivated only by a conception of pleasure and pain has the status of an assumption. Bentham writes, "Nature has placed mankind under the governance of two sovereign masters, *pain* and *pleasure* . . . They govern us in all we do . . . every effort we can make to throw off our subjection, will serve but to demonstrate and confirm it."

(An Introduction to the Principles of Morals and Legislation, Chap. I). In considering what might count as a satisfactory principle of morals, Bentham goes on to say, "The principle of utility recognizes this subjection, and assumes it . . ." (Ibid.). Thus, what Bentham has done is, for the purposes of moral theory, assumed a certain theory of psychological motivation. Now, the theory of motivation that Bentham has assumed clearly rules out Kant's theory of the freedom of the will. But the crucial question has been begged: is freedom of the will possible? Kant's answer, of course, is that freedom is possible, as he argues at great length in the Third Antinomy. There remains, of course, the question whether Kant is successful in demonstrating the possibility of freedom. There is another question, however, which may be of more importance to our present concerns, and it is one which goes to the heart of the issue of the nature of normative moral philosophy: what is to be taken as a starting-point for inquiry in moral theory? How much may be assumed, and what kinds of things are we entitled to assume? Answering this question would take a long time, and I am not prepared to go very far down this road here. Let it suffice to say that it seems inappropriate to make any assumptions about human nature that limit a priori the sorts of principles that may be considered as sound normative principles.

46FMM, p. 417.

47Ibid., p. 419.

48Ibid., p. 394.

49Ibid., pp. 399-400.

50Cf., Ross, Op.cit., p. 73.

51Ibid.

52Cf., Kant, FMM, p. 436.

Chapter III: Legislation and the Distinction
              Between _Wille_ and _Willkür_.

     Having discussed Kant's theories of the
'causality' of the will, we have considered primarily the 'metaphysical' side of his theory of
morals. That is, Kant sees that it is necessary
to 'set the stage' for his normative theory with
an analysis of the nature of the human will, and
of the relation of the will to the world of sense
which is primarily a set of metaphysical assumptions. He believes that he has shown that freedom is possible through his analysis of the Third
Antinomy, and that he has indicated how the will
may be thought of as a 'cause', and as a 'causality'. If this were to be the end of Kant's
moral theory, he would indeed be guilty of committing the 'naturalistic fallacy', as G. E.
Moore charges. However, there is a distinctively
normative side of Kant's moral theory. The concept of legislation is the proper focal point for
a consideration of the normative dimension of
Kant's theory.

     I shall argue that it is because of his view
that moral obligation results from self-legislation that Kant must draw the distinction between
the two senses of 'will' as he does. That is,
Kant's concept of self-legislation can be made
intelligible only in terms of the distinction between _Wille_ and _Willkür_. Not only is legislation
the concept in terms of which we must view Kant's
distinction between the two senses of 'will', but
the distinction serves to account for the very
possibility of autonomous legislation. It is my
view that viewing Kant in his relation to the
tradition of social contract theory makes the distinction between _Wille_ and _Willkür_ intelligible in
a way it would not be otherwise. I shall provide
an analysis of some of the major tenets of contract theory at an appropriate stage.

                        103

A.   The Need for Autonomy.

Kant's reason for insisting that obligation is to be understood as arising from the autonomous will is that this is the only way of conceiving of obligation as sufficiently necessary or absolute.   That is, it is the only way of conceiving of obligation without having to make reference to something outside of oneself.   Any such reference necessarily, for Kant, conditions obligation, and comes under the heading of what Kant terms heteronomy.

Regarding the autonomy of the will, Kant writes,

> Morality is thus the relation
> of actions to the autonomy of
> the will, i.e., to possible
> universal law-giving by maxims
> of the will . . . The dependence
> of a will not absolutely good on
> the principle of autonomy (moral
> constraint) is *obligation*.[1]

The distinction between Wille and Willkür explicates the notion of autonomous legislation and shows the conditions under which such legislation would be possible.   Thus the distinction is crucial for Kant's moral theory because, as we have seen, obligation originates in autonomous legislation.   Wille is the legislator and Willkür is the one to whom the law is legislated.   How is it possible for Wille to legislate?   The answer to this question lies with Kant's analysis of the concept of freedom.   It is tempting to assert that the freedom of the faculty of choice consists in what may be called 'negative freedom', or independence from external determination (spontaneity).[2] As I have noted, though, it would be somewhat misleading to attribute this negative freedom solely to the faculty of choice, as it is the Wille's legislation which provides the kind of 'radical alternative' to desire required to make sense of the absolute spontaneity of the faculty of choice.

It would be a mistake of equal proportion to attribute autonomy solely to the legislative faculty of the will. Indeed, such an attribution would be logically confused, as I shall show. In sum, I shall be arguing that both 'positive' (autonomy) and 'negative' (spontaneity) freedom must be thought of as properties of the combined faculty of the will, including both <u>Wille</u> and <u>Willkür</u>. That is, positive and negative freedom are reciprocal concepts.

1.   Legislation and the Faculty of Choice.

Let us recall some of the earlier discussion of the attributes of the faculty of choice. These remarks will pertain only to the human faculty (as will be obvious once we recall the inapplicability of imperatives of duty to either the holy will or the animal will). In order for the faculty of choice to be bound by autonomous legislation, it must be the case that the human faculty of choice be incompletely determined, though influenced, by some external force, i.e., inclination. Again, in order to be bound by <u>Wille</u>'s legislation, the <u>Willkür</u> must also be independent of complete determination by that legislation. If the faculty of choice were such that it necessarily does that which is required by <u>Wille</u>, then the law would not bind (obligate), but only describe the way the faculty of choice acts.

The above indicates what Kant means in asserting that freedom analytically entails obligation to the moral law.[3] Parenthetically, this also indicates that, for Kant, the concept of freedom has a normative dimension. One is obligated to the moral law arising from one's autonomous will only if one is free in the sense of absolute spontaneity, that is, independent of complete determination by external forces. Kant asserts that reason is 'intrinsically practical', i.e., autonomously legislative. Thus if the faculty of choice is free in the sense of being independent of external determination, then <u>Wille</u> can legislate. If <u>Willkür</u> is such that it could be conceived as constrained by

105

> through the formulation of an
> intrinsically practical and un-
> conditional law. This is its
> real use.[6]

It should be clear that the possibility of reason's
establishing such goals in any meaningful sense
requires two things: (1) that the faculty of
choice be such that it can respond to such goals
once set; (2) that, in order for this setting of
goals to have a normative character, the faculty
of choice be such that it is ultimately independent of this setting of goals, i.e., that it
can be spontaneous.

The crucial distinction between reason in
its 'logical' use and reason in its 'real' use is
that between establishing goals and determining
how goals are to be met, once they have been established. Reason in its 'logical' use is concerned
with the fulfillment of the goals set by inclination. In its 'real' use, reason is concerned to
set goals, rather than to calculate how best to
pursue them. We can see, therefore, that when it
is reason in its 'real' use that is under consideration, the faculty of choice must be independent of
inclination in order to be able to respond to goals
set in the fashion of reason in its 'real' use.

To understand the relation of autonomous legislation to the faculty of choice, we must note
that the faculty of choice is not the source of
the laws by which it chooses to govern its actions.
To be more precise, I suppose that we ought to say
that, if the faculty of choice were the source of
the law governing its actions, then that law would
be arbitrary. Kant writes,

> He who commands (*imperans*) through
> a law is the *lawgiver (legislator)*.
> He is the originator (*auctor*) of
> the obligation imposed by the law,
> but is not always the originator
> of the law. If he is, then the
> law is positive (contingent) and
> arbitrary.[7]

We shall see later that this passage, as well as certain other remarks in the introduction to the Metaphysics of Morals appear to cause some difficulties for Kant's view that obligation originates in autonomous legislation. I think that these problems are merely apparent, however, and I shall attempt to show this at the appropriate juncture.

Since the actions of the faculty of choice presuppose laws, rather than being the source of laws, Kant says that the faculty of choice chooses in accordance with a conception of laws.[8] From this together with the above discussion of the will as a 'causality', it is clear that, when Kant terms the will a 'causality' in the third section of the Grundlegung, he does not have only the faculty of choice in mind but, rather, the combined faculty.[9]

Thus far, we have seen only how it is possible for the faculty of choice to be bound by Wille's legislation. We have not seen the normative dimension of the argument. As I have already indicated, this normative dimension may best be understood in terms of Kant's relations to the tradition of social contract theory. I shall discuss this later.

2.   The Possibility of Hypothetical Imperatives.

One senses that there may be a problem in Kant's entire analysis of the two senses of 'will', and in his conception of the relation between freedom and obligation. If one does not respond to the categorical imperative in one's actions, but responds instead to some hypothetical imperative, what is the source of this imperative?[10] That is, it seems that reason is, for Kant, the source of all imperatives, in the sense that only reason can discern the relations among things in such a way as to be able to tell us how to satisfy a particular inclination (hypothetical imperative) and that only reason can command *a priori* that actions be performed, regardless of their relation to our inclinations. It seems clear that 'rules of skill' and

'counsels of prudence', as Kant calls these hypothetical imperatives,[11] are formulated by reason.
How can it be the case, then, that Kant wants to
assert that one is unconditionally obligated to
the moral law (categorical imperative) if free,
rather than to rules of skill or counsels of prudence (hypothetical imperatives)? What reason is
there to suppose that the law legislated by the
autonomous will must be the categorical imperative, rather than some other law? Kant's answer
to this question, in part, is that hypothetical
imperatives are the result of theoretical rather
than purely practical reason.

In considering the relation between reason
and hypothetical imperatives, Kant's position
resembles that of Hume. Insofar as reason is related to hypothetical imperatives at all, reason
calculates the most effective path to some desired
end.

Of imperatives in general, Kant writes,

> All imperatives are expressed by
> an 'ought' and thereby indicate
> the relation of an objective law
> of reason to a will which is not
> in its subjective constitution
> necessarily determined by this
> law. This relation is that of
> constraint. Imperatives say that
> it would be good to do or to re-
> frain from doing something, but
> they say it to a will which does
> not always do something simply
> because it is presented as a
> good thing to do.[12]

The absolute spontaneity Kant attributes to the
faculty of choice is what accounts for the will's
relation to hypothetical imperatives being an
imperative relation at all. If choice were not
free (spontaneous), we might still act in pursuit
of desire, but not as a response to an imperative.
Rather, the relation between some desired end and

the means necessary to it would be a simple cause/
effect relation (though, as we have seen, Kant's
view of this is far from 'simple'). Freedom of
choice is thus a necessary condition of their
being any imperatives whatever. Wille's legislation of the moral law is necessary if there are
to be actions commanded categorically.

To understand completely the answer Kant must
give to the question why the law legislated by
the autonomous will must be the categorical imperative rather than some other law, it is necessary to understand precisely what is meant by the
term 'autonomous'. The important thing to notice
is that the term implies more than mere independence (that which is captured by the notion of the
faculty of choice as 'spontaneous'). Being 'autonomous'[13] implies a sense of self-legislation, of internal determination.

As noted above, it is important not to confuse
the concept of autonomy with that of the absolute
spontaneity of the faculty of choice. Although
these notions are related in important ways, and
may even be reciprocal concepts, they are disting-
uishable. It is clear from Kant's remarks in
Religion[14] that the spontaneity of the faculty of
choice involves independence, not only from inclination, but from complete determination by the moral
law as well. If the Willkür were not equally independent from the moral law as from inclination,
it might be autonomous, but it could not be conceived as obligated by the principle of autonomy.
Thus the holy will, for which no imperatives hold,
would be autonomous, but not bound by the principle
of autonomy. Thus it is that Kant says that, "The
dependence of a will not absolutely good on the
principle of autonomy (moral constraint) is
obligation."[15]

In saying that the will is autonomous, then,
Kant is asserting that practical reason gives, not
just any law, but its own law, and does not act in
terms of a law of inclination. Saying that reason
gives its own law is crucial, of course, to

110

legislation, i.e., spontaneous, then there is no
question but that <u>Wille</u> will legislate.[4] Here,
in calling the faculty of choice 'free', I mean
what Kant meant in the Third Antinomy, namely,
absolutely spontaneous. I think that, in the
final analysis, this kind of spontaneity is intelligible only in terms of the legislation of
<u>Wille</u>.

It is important to notice, again, that it is
obligation to the moral law that is analytically
entailed by the assumption of freedom, and not
necessarily action in accordance with the moral
law. This underscores once more the independence
of the human faculty of choice from complete determination by the moral law. As Kant says,

> Morality is thus the relation of
> actions to the autonomy of the
> will, i.e., to possible universal
> lawgiving by maxims of the will
> . . . The will whose maxims are
> necessarily in harmony with the
> laws of autonomy is a holy will
> or an absolutely good will. The
> dependence of a will not abso-
> lutely good on the principle of
> autonomy (moral constraint) is
> *obligation*.[5]

It is important to note this last point, because it suggests that 'intrinsically practical
reason' is a notion which refers to the entire
rational faculty of the will, and not to <u>Wille</u>
alone, as one might expect. To see this, let us
note, again, what is meant in terming reason 'intrinsically practical'. Once again, I shall rely
on Beck's interpretation:

> Reason is concerned not with the
> choice among ways to some end pro-
> jected by desire; this is its
> merely logical use. It estab-
> lishes the goals of action

understanding what kind of law it must be that is
legislated by the autonomous will. A law which
could come from reason alone can have no reference to anything that is other than reason. A
law such as this, if it is to be legislated, or
made an imperative of duty, can therefore make
no reference to anything empirical. That this
is Kant's contention is clear:

> . . . here is it a question of
> objectively practical laws and
> thus of the relation of a will
> to itself so far as it determines
> itself only by reason; for every-
> thing which has a relation to the
> empirical automatically falls away,
> because if reason of itself alone
> determines conduct, it must neces-
> sarily do so a priori.[16]

The reference in the above passage to the
'*a priori* determination' of conduct is, in itself, rather misleading. It sounds as if Kant is
saying that what we do is somehow decided before-
hand, which would result, of course, in a blatant
contradiction with the entire thrust of his moral
theory. Our discussion of the two senses of 'will',
however, points out what Kant means by 'determination' in this instance, and shows it to be consistent with his general view.

B.   Kant's Theory of Moral Legislation.

As I have already noted, it may be objected
that there is nothing obviously normative about anything said in either the chapter on the 'causality'
of the will, or the present chapter up to this
point. Indeed there is not. The causal analysis
is necessary, if one is to make sense of several of
the things Kant says about the will, particularly
the possibility of Willkür causing actions in the
world of sense, and Wille's determination of the
faculty of choice. It is necessary that we understand these things, in order to understand what it
is to which we are obligated if Kant's normative

111

theory can be vindicated. The question remains: why ought we to let our choices be guided by the law legislated by Wille? I have previously suggested that, in this connection, Kant's concept of legislation is a crucial notion in his theory of moral obligation. Some of the characteristics of the concept of legislation have already been mentioned. The purpose of the present section is to analyze the concept of legislation in more detail and to show its importance for Kant's overall moral theory. To accomplish this task, the following topics must be discussed: (1) the concept of legislation and the distinction between internal and external legislation; (2) the role of the concept of legislation in Kant's theory of moral obligation; (3) the relation between Kant's concept of legislation and his notion of the free will; (4) an analysis of the central questions of the Grundlegung in terms of the concept of legislation. I shall argue throughout that the concept of legislation is the central concept in Kant's theory of obligation, and that other key notions in his moral theory may best be understood in terms of their relation to the concept of legislation.

1.   The Distinction Between Internal and External Legislation.

To appreciate the merit of the assertion that legislation is the central concept in Kant's moral theory, it is necessary to understand the concept as Kant uses it. The German term which is translated as 'legislation' is *Gesetzgebung*. Kant's use of this term is itself illuminating: literally translated, the term means 'a giving of law'. It would be a gross misinterpretation to suppose that 'legislation' refers to statutes, or anything of the like. Understanding 'legislation' as referring to statutes would lead us to think that legislation is something essentially passive. Kant understands legislation as an active concept, as his use of the term *Gesetzgebung* indicates.

Legislation is, for Kant, a complex notion, consisting of two elements: (1) a law making the

112

action in question a duty; (2) an incentive to perform the action.[17]   Two kinds of legislation are
distinguished according to the kind of incentive
involved.   Ethical (internal) legislation makes
the fact that the action is taken to be a duty the
incentive for doing the action.   Juridicial (external) legislation makes something other than the
idea of duty the incentive.   For instance, the
agent might elect to fulfill the terms of a contract for fear of imprisonment, rather than because he or she felt a duty to abide by the terms
of the contract.

The following will help to illustrate further
the distinction between the two kinds of legislation: agreement of an action with the law, when
the nature of the incentive to perform the action
is not considered, is the legality of the action;
". . . when the Idea of duty arising from the law
is at the same time the incentive of the action,
then the agreement is called the morality of the
action."[18]   The morality of an action involves
making the fact of the action's being a duty the
reason for performing the action.

The relation of these remarks to the position
Kant takes in the Grundlegung regarding the notion
of moral worth is clear.   Kant writes,

> . . . it is a duty to preserve
> one's life, and moreover everyone
> has a direct inclination to do so.
> But for that reason the often
> anxious care which most men take of
> it has no intrinsic worth, and the
> maxim of doing so has no moral import.
> They preserve their lives according
> to duty, but not from duty.[19]

Are these two kinds of legislation altogether
independent of one another?   They are not, for the
following reason: ". . . ethical legislation also
makes internal actions duties, but does not, however, exclude external actions; rather, it applies

113

generally to everything that is a duty."[20] Thus
any duty whatever may be legislated internally,
or ethically.[21] Of these duties, some, but not
all, can also be legislated juridically, or externally.

I think that we should probably say 'can
appropriately be legislated juridically' here,
to make clear that Kant's theory of legislation
is a theory of normative obligation. By this I
mean that there are some actions which, though I
ought morally to perform them, I should not (and
in some instances cannot) be coerced legally into
performing them. To take an example, and perhaps
a controversial one at that, I would say that it
is appropriate legally that one be made not to
discriminate in hiring practices. It is, further,
appropriate morally that one not discriminate
simply for the reason that one has a duty to treat
all persons equally. It is clear, however, that it
is not possible legally to coerce someone to refrain from discrimination on any particular grounds.
To take another case, it is appropriate morally
that I stop to help someone in distress, but it is
not clear that it is appropriate legally that I be
coerced, under pain of fine or imprisonment, into
doing so. The first example is an instance in
which it is not possible to coerce someone legally,
the second a case in which it is possible but not
proper.

It should be clear that, for Kant, it is
never possible to legislate externally actions
having moral worth. The moral worth of actions
has to do with the motive from which they are done,
and it is the free faculty of choice that determines
the motive. Thus, no motive can ever be legislated
externally. As regards the 'material' of the action,
of course, it may always be possible, at least in
principle, to coerce a person externally into doing
the action. But I do not think that Kant would
want to call this a case of external legislation,
if the act which someone was coerced to perform
could not be a duty in the first place. Legislation
is an activity by which we become bound to actions,

114

and, in the case of the legislation of the moral law, to law itself.

The foregoing immediately raises a difficulty, one posed by R. P. Wolff: does not Kant commit himself to being a 'philosophical anarchist' through his remarks about autonomous legislation?[22] I do not think that it is the case that Kant is thus committed, even philosophically, but I shall leave the discussion of this point to the concluding chapter, in which I intend to address a variety of 'lingering difficulties'.

The above remarks require, I think, some amplification of the concept of external legislation, and of the relation between internal and external legislation. There are innumerable actions which one might, in one fashion or another, be gotten to perform, but Kant is not about to class all of these actions as duties. He writes, "The dependence of a will not absolutely good on the principle of autonomy (moral constraint) is *obligation* . . . The objective necessity of an action from obligation is called duty."[23] Or, "Duty is that action to which a person is bound. It is therefore the content [Materie] of obligation. And there can be one and the same duty (so far as the action is concerned), even though we could be obligated thereto in different ways."[24]

I mentioned earlier that Kant seems to use the term 'maxim' ambiguously, meaning, on some occasions, the entire subjective principle of action, including a reference to motive, and at other junctures the 'content' of the principle, the action itself viewed as independent of motive. There may be a similar ambiguity present regarding Kant's use of the notion of duty, which can include the type of legislation through which one is bound, or can refer only to the action itself, independently of the type of legislation. I think that, for the most part, Kant is careful to distinguish between *Pflicht* (duty) and *Art der Verpflichtung* (way of being bound to a duty). In any event, he

certainly takes more care to maintain this distinction than he does with that between the two
senses of 'maxim'.

I take it that internal and external legislation are two different ways in which one might be
bound to actions. Notice, now, that, since both
forms of legislation share the element of a law
making the action in question a duty, no one can
be bound to do that which conflicts with laws of
duty. This is the case, despite the quite obvious fact that one can be coerced into doing something that is in conflict with objective practical
laws. This being the case, though, it seems to be
quite clear that the concept of legislation,
whether internal or external, is a normative concept, referring to that which it is appropriate
for an individual to be coerced or constrained to
do, whether that constraint be internally or externally applied.

This last point is quite important, so let
me try to clarify it by putting it in another
fashion. While it is true that one can be externally coerced into doing something inappropriate, one ought not to be. Also, while one can
persuade oneself to do something inappropriate,
one ought not to do so. In refusing to call
either of these cases instances of 'legislation',
Kant would be underscoring the normative dimension of the concept of legislation.

It may be thought that the last point is in
conflict with Kant's views of the spontaneity of
the faculty of choice. I do not think this is
the case, although I see why it might be thought
to do so. I think that when Kant speaks of individuals being 'coerced' into performing actions,
he does not mean for us to understand anything so
final as to rule out our refusing to respond to
the coercion. To 'coerce' here means something
much closer to 'offer an incentive' and the distinction between internal and external 'coercion',
once again, is that between duty and external

incentives (e.g., pleasures or pains, either promised or threatened). As the possibility of refusing to accept the 'coercion' always remains open, there is no conflict with Kant's doctrine of the absolute spontaneity of the faculty of choice.

Let us examine the concept of external legislation more closely. What, exactly, is external legislation? The paradigm example involves the concept of a valid legal contract. If two parties have entered into a valid contract, it is appropriate for either party to take legal action to force the other party to comply with the terms of said contract. Thus an incentive, the appeal to self-interested generated by, say, the threat of fine or imprisonment, other than the idea of duty itself is applied to coerce the parties into abiding by the terms of the contract. Rather, we should say, it would be appropriate that such coercion be applied.

Surely, the parties to the contract ought to abide by the terms without having to have the external threats as incentives. But here two points are relevant: it is nevertheless appropriate for the aggrieved party to apply the external constraints (through legal means); it is not appropriate, and, indeed, not even intelligible for one to speak of coercing an individual externally to adopt the idea of duty as an incentive. This would be a clear contradiction in terms. External legislation refers specifically to incentives other than the idea of duty.

If external legislation can be characterized as external coercion, then, presumably, internal legislation would have to be internal coercion, or self-coercion. This is true, but it is an incomplete statement of Kant's notion of internal legislation. I can coerce myself to do that which I perceive to be in my own interest, but this would not count as an act of internal legislation. It would not because the idea of duty is not taken as the incentive. Kant's analysis of freedom, both in the Grundlegung, and in the Critiques, is designed to show, not that I can move myself to pursue my own interest, but, rather, that I can move myself to action for reasons having no bearing on my sensuous interest, or without consideration of that interest.

2. The Relation Between Internal and External Legislation

What is the relation between internal and external legislation? It is decidedly not the case that the entire class of duties can be parceled out, some falling to internal legislation, others to external legislation. Kant writes,

> Suppose there were no such duties
> [duties to oneself]. Then there
> would be no duties at all, not
> even external ones. For I cannot
> recognize myself as bound to others
> except insofar as I bind myself at
> the same time: the law by virtue
> of which I regard myself as bound
> arises in all cases from my own
> practical reason, through which I
> am constrained while being at the
> same time the one who constrains.[25]

Thus, there can be no obligations at all unless there is internal obligation, which is possible only if there is internal legislation.[26] This appears to assert the primacy of internal legislation over external legislation, and this primacy must be examined and explained.

Is internal legislation necessary in order that an action be a duty? In order that particular actions be duties, it is not necessary that those actions be internally legislated, i.e., that the idea of duty be taken as the incentive for performing those actions. For example, preserving one's own life, Kant would say, is a duty.[27] It is a duty, furthermore, no matter what reason (incentive) one follows in preserving one's life. Indeed, it is a duty whether one abides by it or not. We shall see later that there is something seemingly paradoxical about Kant's conception of legislation: on one hand, legislation is that act through which one comes to be bound to perform particular actions, and involves the adoption of an incentive (motive); on the other, it is possible for one to fail to perform actions to which one is bound. It will be necessary to draw a distinction between being bound to a particular action, and being bound to a law. The former presupposes the latter.

Also, it is necessary to recognize something fundamental about the 'incentive' component in Kant's concept of legislation. There is a distinction between something's being an incentive for action and its being my incentive. Thus, I can be bound to an action or a law without its being the case that I necessarily perform the act. Indeed, how could the case be otherwise, if Kant is to have a normative theory at all?

The sense in which internal legislation is necessary for all duty is the following: it must be *possible*, in the case of any duty, that that duty be internally legislated. That is, it must be possible to choose to do a given action solely because it is a duty.

It is important to notice here some significant relations between the present discussion and the earlier analysis of maxims and motives in connection with the faculty of choice. In the latter instance, I pointed out that, for Kant, the concept of a maxim (in the fullest sense of the term) contained a reference to the motive. Two maxims might result in the same concrete action, considered externally. The maxims might nevertheless be distinguished in terms of motive. For instance, take Kant's famous example of the 'prudent merchant':

> . . . it is in fact in accord-
> ance with duty that a dealer
> should not overcharge an inex-
> perienced customer, and wherever
> there is much business the prudent
> merchant does not do so . . . But
> this is far from sufficient to
> justify the belief that the mer-
> chant has behaved in this way from
> duty and principles of morality.
> His own advantage required this
> behavior; . . .[28]

Kant's point, of course, is that, though the external result is the same--the customer is honestly
served--the maxims are in one sense quite different. Kant, of course, speaks in this same way,
regarding the distinction between external and
internal legislation.

It is part of Kant's view of the nature of
the relationship between internal and external
legislation that all duties may be legislated
internally while only some may be legislated
externally. Perhaps we should pause briefly to
consider whether we are prepared to agree with
Kant on this. That this is Kant's view seems to
be clear: "Ethical legislation is that which cannot be external (though the duties may be external); juridical legislation is that which can
also be external."[29] Here, Kant seems to say that
there is some legislation, namely, ethical legislation, which cannot be external. Further, he
says,

> Thus, to keep one's promise in a
> contract is an external duty; but
> the command to do so merely be-
> cause it is a duty, without regard
> to any other incentive, belongs
> only to internal legislation.[30]

Now, insofar as the action itself is concerned,
there can be no distinction between keeping a contract from duty and keeping the same contract

from a motive of self-interest. Thus, in this respect, it may appear that the same actions, considered in abstraction from the motive to performance of the action, are required by both internal and external legislation. So far as external duties (duties to others) are concerned, this is what one would expect. So far as internal duties are concerned, though, the situation seems rather different. We generally take it to be wrong (morally) to take one's own life, and we furthermore impose legal sanctions against--though, obviously enough, the sanctions can only be applied to those who attempt suicide and fail. But, though we may also take it to be morally wrong for perople to refuse to educate themselves, it is clear that we feel that we are rather limited as regards the sorts of legal action we think it appropriate to take against those who reject education. True enough, society does attempt to provide incentives and to encourage those who might otherwise not seek to educate themselves. But this scarcely seems like legislation as Kant appears to have intended that notion. He seems to mean the notion of 'incentive' in this connection in the sense of a threat of something unpleasant that will happen if one fails to comply--again, the paradigm of the fine or imprisonment if one fails to live up to the terms of a contract. We should grant, of course, that the notion of an 'incentive' can be much broader than that of a 'threat'. Nevertheless, the notion of 'threat' seems to be what Kant had in mind.

Thus it appears that we should say that the category of duties that can be legislated internally is a broader one than that of externally legislated duties in two respects: (1) insofar as the concept of the incentive to perform the action is included, no internal duty can be legislated externally, though any external duty can be legislated internally (done for duty's sake); (2) in the case of some duties ('imperfect' duties to oneself, I think), even the action itself without regard to motive cannot properly be legislated externally,

121

that is, we ought not to threaten people into
undertaking projects of self-improvement.

Let us examine the concept of internal legislation more closely. The possibility of choosing
to do an action solely because it is a duty involves two things: (1) the action in question
must be a duty in the first place; (2) the will
which chooses to perform the action must be free.[31]
It ought not to be thought that these two elements
are independent of each other. To the contrary,
they reciprocally involve each other. If one is
not free, in the sense of being able to act independently of external factors determining one
to act, it makes no sense to speak of there being
any duties at all. That is, if the way we act is
not in some sense up to us, it is nonsensical to
say that we ought to act in certain ways. One is
put in mind immediately of Kant's remarks concerning the holy will: ". . . no imperatives
hold for the divine will or, more generally, for
a holy will. The 'ought' is here out of place,
for the volition of itself is necessarily in
unison with the law."[32] On the other hand, however, if there were no objective demands being
made upon the will, it would make no sense to say
the will is free. Being free seems to involve
being able to act out of some motivation other
than the mere serving of some passionate interest.
Again, the concept of reason in its 'real' use is
relevant to understanding the point here. As Beck
writes, "It [reason] establishes the goals of
action through the formulation of an intrinsically
practical and unconditional law. This is its real
use."[33] Thus we can see that it is impossible to
say that freedom and duty are independent notions.
There can be no duty unless we are free, but neither
can there be any real freedom unless there is duty.
It is simply impossible to make sense of either of
these notions without reference to the other.

It should also be noted that, although external
legislation relies on an incentive other than duty,
precisely the same conditions that make internal

legislation possible are the conditions of the possibility of external legislation. That is, both forms of legislation share the element of law and, furthermore, since we should never speak of one as bound by external legislation except insofar as it is possible for one to refuse to live up to what that legislation requires, it seems that the freedom of the will presupposed in internal legislation is a requirement for external legislation as well.

3. Utilitarian Conceptions of Internal and External Sanctions.

It may help us to come to a clearer understanding of Kant's distinction between internal and external legislation, if we contrast his view with the distinction in utilitarian moral theories between internal and external sanctions. Bentham, Hume, and J. S. Mill are the utilitarian theorists whose views come most immediately to mind, and I shall discuss each of them briefly here.

a. Bentham.

In his Introduction to the Principles of Morals and Legislation, Bentham distinguishes four 'sanctions'. He writes,

> There are four distinguishable
> sources from which pleasure and
> pain are in use to flow: con-
> sidered separately, they may be
> termed the *physical*, the *political*,
> the *moral*, and the *religious*: and
> inasmuch as the pleasures and pains
> belonging to each of them are capa-
> ble of giving a binding force to
> any law or rule of conduct, they
> may all of them be termed sanctions.[34]

In a footnote to this discussion, Bentham notes, "Sanctio, in Latin, was used to signify the *act of binding*, and, by a common grammatical transition, *any thing which serves to bind a man*:"[35]

123

Sanctions, then, are sources of motives, of pains and pleasures which are, for Bentham, the only things that can move a person to do anything whatever.[36]

It is Bentham's concept of the political sanction that appears to come closest to Kant's notion of external legislation:

> If at the hands of a *particular* person or set of persons in the community, who under names correspondent to that of *judge*, are chosen for the particular purpose of dispensing it [the pleasure or pain], according to the will of the sovereign or supreme ruling power in the state, it again, the pleasure or pain may be said to issue from the *political sanction*.[37]

Bentham is speaking here of what would have to be called the 'incentive component' of Kant's concept of legislation. It should not be thought, however, that Bentham's position contains no reference whatever to the 'law component' of Kant's position. Bentham writes, "It has been shown that the happiness of the individuals of whom a community is composed . . . is the end and the sole end which the legislator ought to have in view: the sole standard, in conformity to which each individual ought, . . . to be made to fashion his behaviour."[38] Thus, Bentham believes that he has already established utility as the principle of conduct (law) to which individuals are to be bound; the only task remaining being that of accounting for the various ways in which individuals can be bound to the principle of utility. While it would be an interesting and worthwhile undertaking this is not the place to investigate the adequacy of Bentham's establishment of utility.

While the law or principle involved in Bentham's theory of legislation would, for obvious reasons, make Kant unhappy (no pun intended), there is a

resemblance between Bentham's 'political sanction' and Kant's external incentive'. There seems
to be no corresponding resemblance between Kant's
'internal incentive' and any of Bentham's other
sanctions, however. What Bentham calls the 'moral
sanction' turns out, on inspection, to be nothing
more than public opinion.[39] It is the case, of
course, that each individual has to, as it were,
'internalize' the pressure of public opinion, if
that sanction is to have any effect, but this is
scarcely the 'absolute spontaneity' of the faculty
of choice of which Kant speaks. For Kant, the
'internal incentive' involves the possibility of
making the idea of duty the incentive for action.
In Bentham's case, the 'moral sanction' still involves the use of pleasures and pains as means
of coercing individuals into action. The source
of the pleasure and pain is now, as Bentham says,
". . . such *chance* persons in the community, as
the party in question may happen in the course of
his life to have concerns with, . . ."[40], rather
than those authorized individuals designated by
the community, as in the case of the political
sanction.

At the risk of grossly oversimplifying the
case, I would like to suggest what I take to be
the main root of the distinction between Bentham
and Kant: Bentham assumes an empirical theory of
human motivation, taking human nature to be such
that we can be moved only by pleasure and pain,
and then asks what principle(s) of morals can be
maintained under this assumption; Kant, on the
other hand, begins with what he takes to be the
shared common-sense conceptions of the unconditional character of moral obligation, and proceeds to ask what we would have to assume about
human nature in order to 'vindicate' our common-
sense conceptions. Kant is led, in following
this course, to deal with the question of human
motivation. Thus, both Kant and Bentham deal in
due course with the same issues, but in a very
different order. It seems to me, as I indicated

125

earlier, that in this instance, the difference in order accounts for the bulk of the difference between the two thinkers. Of course, the difference in order is itself accounted for by other differences between Bentham and Kant in terms of their general philosophical orientation, and so on, but this would not be the place to engage in a lengthy discussion of these matters. I think that Kant has put the theory of motivation in its proper place, but this, too, is a matter worthy of separate treatment. There is unfortunately not time for it here.

b.   Hume.

David Hume's Inquiry Concerning the Principles of Morals is one of the most sophisticated pieces of utilitarian moral theory ever written, if in fact Hume is really a utilitarian at all, which I think there is some reason to doubt. Hume's theory of incentives is in some ways more sophisticated than Bentham's. For this reason, I have chosen to discuss Hume after Bentham, even though Hume's writing pre-dates Bentham's by a number of years.[41]

Hume's theory of motivation has two facets: (1) his distinction between 'self-love' and 'benevolence' as the grounds moving us to approve or disapprove of certain actions, in ourselves or in others; (2) he raises the question of the ground of our obligation to benevolence. In the former regard, Hume's position is not altogether unlike Kant's. In the latter, Hume appears to be at odds with Kant, though I think that the real gap between them is narrower than it is commonly taken to be.

Hume's distinction between grounds of approval and incentives for action is of great importance to his theory. Having observed that we do approve of actions that are beneficial to persons other than ourselves, he proceeds to inquire how this can be the case. He writes, "We must adopt a more public affection and allow that the interests of society are not, *even on their own account*, entirely indifferent to us."[42] The important point here is

126

that approval of actions can flow directly from
a perception of benefit to others, without having
to be mediated by any perception of benefit to
ourselves.

Up to a point, I think that Kant would agree
with Hume. Kant certainly feels that it is necessary to account for our approval of actions having
no bearing on our own personal interest. Where
Kant and Hume seem bound to part company is on
the question, not of what kinds of actions can
gain our approval, but of how we can be moved to
perform actions having our approval.

For Kant, as we have seen, morality is possible only if there can be a source of incentives
to action other than self-interest. While Hume
apparently feels that there is a source of *approval*
other than self-interest, he seems to recognize no
other origin of incentives to action. Hume writes,

> Having explained the moral
> *approvation* attending merit or
> virtue, there remains nothing
> but briefly to consider our
> interested *obligation*, and to
> inquire whether every man who
> has any regard to his own happi-
> ness and welfare will not best
> find his account in the practice
> of every moral duty.[43]

Hume concludes, of course, that we must be able to
argue that being moral (benevolent) is, in the last
analysis, in our own true interest. He says, ". . .
what theory of morals can ever serve any useful
purpose unless it can show, by a particular detail,
that all the duties which it recommends are also
the true interest of each individual?"[44] Thus,
it is Hume's view that we can, finally, be moved
to virtue only because we conceive our own true
interest to be bound up with being moral. This
would seem not to do for Kant, but I believe that
these positions are not so divergent as they seem.

127

Kant distinguishes between 'having an interest' and 'taking an interest'. If morality is to be possible, it must be the case that we can taken an interest in the moral law, i.e., bind ourselves to it. It must be equally impossible that we can bind ourselves to the law only because we think we have an interest in it. Kant says,

> . . . why should I subject myself as a rational being, and thereby all other beings endowed with reason, to this law? I will admit that *no interest impels me* to do so, for that would then give no categorical imperative. But I must nevertheless *take an interest in it*,[45]

And, further,

> We do find sometimes that we can take an interest in a personal quality which involves no [personal] interest in any [external] condition, provided only that [possession of] this quality makes us capable of participating in the [desired] condition . . . That is, mere worthiness to be happy even without the motive of participating in it can interest us of itself. But this judgment is in fact only the effect of the already assumed importance of moral laws . . .[46]

Now, surely, Kant's position is the antithesis of Hume's on the subject of morality and self-interest. Not so, in my view. Recall that, when Hume speaks of our interest in morality, he refers to our 'true' interest, and not to mere self-love. It is not a prospect of personal gain that binds us to morality and, for this reason, the positions of Hume and Kant are in reality not poles apart as one might think.

c.   J. S. Mill.

Mill's <u>Utilitarianism</u> is perhaps the most
widely read piece of utilitarian moral theory to
appear since Kant's own writings (decidedly non-
utilitarian, clearly). Mill has a clear conception of what I think is the central issue of
normative moral philosophy: how can we be bound
to principles of morality? Mill writes,

> The question is often asked, and
> properly so, in regard to any sup-
> posed moral standard--What is its
> sanction? What are the motives to
> obey? or, more specifically, what
> is the source of its obligation?
> whence does it derive its binding
> force? . . . why am I bound to pro-
> mote the general happiness? If my
> own happiness lies in something
> else, why may I not give that the
> preference?[47]

Mill's views have been criticized frequently, and
he has even been accused of making rather simplistic
logical blunders.[48] I think, in fact, that Mill's
view is (1) more sophisticated in several respects
than that of either Bentham or Hume, and (2) closer
to Kant's position than is generally recognized.

Unlike Bentham, for whom all sanctions appear
to have their ultimate origin outside of the individual, Mill recognizes the possibility of a
genuinely internal sanction. Of external sanctions,
Mill writes, "Of the external sanctions it is not
necessary to speak at any length. They are the
hope of favor and the fear of displeasure from our
fellow creatures or from the Ruler of the universe
. . ."[49] Here, Mill seems to have captured and
grouped together Bentham's political, moral and
religious sanctions. It is in the case of internal
sanctions that Mill differs from Bentham. Mill
says,

> The internal sanction of duty,
> whatever our standard of duty
> may be, is one and the same--a
> feeling in our own mind; a pain,
> more or less intense, attendant on
> violation of duty . . . This feel-
> ing, when disinterested and con-
> necting itself with the pure idea
> of duty, . . . is the essence of
> conscience;[50]

Not only is Mill's internal sanction genuinely internal, but it is also disinterested, by which Mill appears to mean that it has no immediate bearing on one's own self-interest. Is this in conflict with Mill's assertion that the internal sanction is a feeling, a pain? I think not. I can think some action worth performing, and in fact perform the action, without having to think that the consequences of performing the action will do me any good.

I think Bentham also believes that we can be moved to perform actions which we perceive as having no bearing on our self-interest. The difference between Mill and Bentham on this point is that, for Mill, the incentive to perform such actions may be genuinely internal, while for Bentham this seems not to be the case.

There also appears to be an interesting contrast between Mill and Hume on an important point: Mill seems to think that there can be genuine conflict between the requirements of morality and one's own self-interest, while Hume seems ultimately not to recognize such a conflict. Mill writes, " . . . why am I bound to promote the general happiness? If my own happiness lies in something else, why may I not give that the preference?"[51] This seems to suggest that it is at least possible that my interest and the requirements of the general happiness might be at odds. Hume, on the other hand, says,

130

> Having explained the moral
> *approbation* attending merit
> or virtue, there remains nothing
> but briefly to consider our in-
> terested *obligation* to it, and
> to inquire whether every man who
> has any regard to his own happi-
> ness and welfare will not best
> find his account in the practice
> of every moral duty.[52]

Hume's conclusion, as we have already noted, is that it must be the case that morality conduces to the individual's own true interest, else it would be impossible to motivate people to act morally.[53] Recall, though, that there is a distinction between mere self-interest and 'true' interest. I am led by this fact to conclude that the apparent contrast between Mill and Hume is merely apparent.

Mill's position, I think, is closer to our own intuitions about morals than is the view of Bentham. Bentham seems to presuppose an empirical theory of motivation and tries to build a moral theory around it. Mill attempts, I think, to be more faithful to the data of ordinary moral experience, chief among which is the intuition that there are some actions that we ought to perform, regardless of their impact on our own interests, at least where 'interest' is understood as mere self-interest.

I think that Kant would agree with Mill on at least two counts: (1) that morality requires not only that we be able to approve of actions having no bearing on our interest, but also that we be capable of being moved to perform such actions; (2) that morality requires a genuinely internal sanction, and not merely a variety of external sanctions.

Kant would also disagree with Mill on at least two counts, however, one of which is of special

131

importance to the concerns of the present chapter. The two counts are: (1) the principle of utility can never, in Kant's view, bind us categorically, as a moral law must; (2) to be a truly moral incentive, the internal sanction cannot be grounded on pain, even if this be a pain arising in the mind, rather than one being externally imposed. It is this latter objection to Mill that is of special interest here. Let us examine it before returning to the main lines of our inquiry.

Kant would argue that, although we may indeed feel pain upon the contemplation of violation of duty, we will not have acted morally, our action will have no moral worth, if we take the avoidance of this pain as our incentive for acting. This would yield only an hypothetical imperative, never a categorical one. And Kant seems indeed to be right about this because, as Mill himself says, ". . . this sanction has no binding efficacy on those who do not possess the feelings it appeals to . . ."[54]

C.   The Role of the Concept of Legislation in Kant's Theory of Moral Obligation.

The purpose of the preceding section has been to see how the question of the incentives to morality is treated by representatives of a kind of moral theory Kant criticizes, and to understand something of Kant's criticisms. We must turn now to a discussion of the role of the concept of legislation in Kant's theory of moral obligation. Necessarily, the nature of the concept of legislation itself will be drawn out in more detail in this section.

1.   The Possibility of Internal Legislation.

Since the possibility of internal legislation is ultimately the ground of the possibility of there being any duty whatsoever, the question of how internal legislation is possible is an important one. What is the relation between legislation and obligation? To say that a duty is 'legislated'

132

carries the connotation that (1) the duty has the force of law behind it, and (2) there is a two-party relation involved, consisting of a legislator and someone to whom the duty is legislated. Kant writes, "He who commands *(imperans)* through a law is the *lawgiver (legislator)*. He is the originator *(auctor)* of the obligation . . . but is not always the originator of the law."[55]

Thus it is that obligation originates with the act of legislation. The emphasis upon the legislator as the originator of the obligation imposed by the law is an important point. If the law could not be legislated, there could be no obligation. In its relation to human beings, it does not even seem to make sense to speak of the moral law as 'existing' if it could not be legislated. Since the moral law is, for Kant, an unconditional and intrinsically practical law, it must necessarily have a relation to conduct, the moral law could exist as a descriptive law for a holy will, even if it were the case that there were no free rational beings to be bound by it. But then it would scarcely be a moral law at all. In the case of human beings, the relation of the moral law to conduct is a normative relation, binding us to perform certain actions. From this it follows that it is of the essence of the moral law that, given the existence of free rational beings, it will be legislated.

It should be recalled at this point that Kant draws a distinction between obligation *(Verbindlichkeit)* and duty *(Pflicht)*. He appears to keep rather strictly to the distinction throughout his ethical writings.[56] The distinction between the meanings of the two terms is illuminating.

Verbindlichkeit is the noun derived from the verb *verbinden* which means, literally, 'to tie' or 'to bind'. *Verbindlichkeit*, then, means a 'state of being bound'--in the case of Kant's moral philosophy, bound to the moral law. Obligation is thus an active concept for Kant, and does not refer to particular actions which any agent should perform. In our ordinary language, we frequently use the terms 'duty' and 'obligation' interchangeably, as if they were exact synonyms. Kant, however, maintains a distinction.

Pflicht is the German term which is translated as 'duty'. This term, unlike Kant's use of 'obligation', does refer to concrete actions which the individual ought to perform. Thus, *Pflicht* refers to actions, or, rather, to an individual's relation to possible actions, while *Verbindlichkeit* refers to the individual's relation to the moral law.

When one ascribes to Kant the position that obligation is general, applying equally to all rational beings, it is important to see that this refers to obligation and thus to the relation of individuals to the moral law, and not to duty, or the individual's relation to possible actions. Kant is surely not committed to the absurd position that all individuals have precisely the same concrete duties to perform.

Let us return to the central question of this section, and raise a number of questions regarding the role of internal legislation in Kant's theory of obligation. First, I shall examine Kant's assertion that legislation is the origin of obligation. Second, given that legislation is a two-party relation, I shall ask what or who are the parties that comprise an act of legislation (it will be seen that this question may be linked to the two elements contained in the concept of legislation). Third, with regard to the second question, I shall examine the possibility of duty being the incentive of the will. The last two questions may be seen as related to the central questions of the Grundlegung. Fourth, I shall discuss the relation between the two elements in legislation, and the way these two elements are related to obligation. This last discussion serves to indicate the kind of theory of obligation Kant is proposing.

134

2.   Legislation as the Origin of Obligation.

Kant's primary interest throughout most of his ethical writings is with the possibility of obligation in general, rather than with the discussion of particular duties, although he does of course deal with this later. This point is underscored in Kant's remark, "*Duty* is that action to which a person is bound. It is therefore the content (*Materie*) of obligation."[57] Obligation, then, concerns the binding of persons not to particular actions, but to principles of action. This has been shown in the discussion of Kant's concept of *Verbindlichkeit*. What kind of 'binding' is Kant considering? He says, ". . . duty is practical unconditional necessity of action; it must, therefore, hold for all rational beings (. . .), and only for that reason can it be a law for all human wills."[58] The kind of obligation for which we are seeking the conditions, then, is unconditional obligation. That is, we are seeking the conditions of obligation that makes categorical demands.

What kind of legislation is required for unconditional obligation? It is clear that Kant takes autonomous legislation to be the kind of legislation required for unconditional obligation. What is the autonomy of the will? It is that property of the will, ". . . by which it is a law to itself independently of any property of objects of volition."[59] Legislation is, as we have seen, a giving of law.[60] Autonomous legislation, then, is a giving of law that proceeds independently of any objects of volition, that is, without reference to inclination.

It is clear from these remarks that autonomous legislation must be internal. External legislation, since it takes something other than the idea of duty as the incentive for action, cannot be autonomous.

Why must legislation establishing absolute obligation necessarily originate in autonomous

legislation, independently of any objects of volition?[61] To be absolute, or unconditional, means
that the obligation (not necessarily the duty) will
apply equally and of necessity to all free rational
beings. If the legislation establishing obligation were determined by objects of volition (things
one happened to desire), then the obligation thereby established would apply to persons only under
the condition that they shared the desire for the
particular object. This is true even of those
things we necessarily desire, because of the nature
of our subjective constitution. Even though that
which we necessarily desire is a partial source
of what Kant calls imperfect duty, these desires
are not the ultimate foundations of all obligation.
The ultimate conditions of the existence of any
obligation whatever are the conditions of perfect
duty: the existence of free rational beings.[62]

These assertions regarding the concept of
'necessary desire' and Kant's distinction between
perfect and imperfect duties stand in need of some
further discussion. This will shed some light on
Kant's views about autonomous legislation as the
origin of categorical obligation.

Kant's distinction between perfect and imperfect duties is, by now, quite notorious. Kant
presents four examples of maxims that are alleged
to be contrary to duty, in order both to illustrate
the distinction between perfect and imperfect duties
and to clarify what he would have us understand by
the notion of the 'universalizability' of a maxim.[63]
I do not intend to undertake a full-scale investi-
gation either of Kant's four examples or of the
distinction between perfect and imperfect duties
here, though I have discussed these matters elsewhere.[64] Rather, I shall be content here to eluci-
date the relation between desire and imperfect duty,
insofar as this is relevant to the present concerns.

Of the distinction between perfect and imperfect duties itself, Kant writes,

> Some actions are of such a nature
> that their maxims cannot even be
> *thought* as a universal law without
> contradiction, far from it being
> possible that one could will that
> it should be such. In others this
> internal impossibility is not
> found, though it is still impos-
> sible to will that their maxim
> should be raised to the universality
> of a law of nature, because such a
> will would contradict itself. We
> easily see that the former maxim
> conflicts with the stricter or nar-
> rower (imprescriptible) duty, the
> latter with broader (meritorious)
> duty.[65]

Thus Kant begins to draw the distinction between
perfect and imperfect duty in terms of actions
whose maxims cannot even be thought universally
without contradiction, and those acts whose maxims
can be thought but not willed universally without
contradiction. Kant characterizes the 'contradictions' that are alleged to arise in attempting
to universalize actions whose maxims involve violations of duty as internal (violations of perfect
duty) and external (violations of imperfect duty).

Let us focus on one of Kant's examples of a
violation of imperfect duty, in order to see more
clearly how desire and duty are related. Consider
Kant's example of the proposed maxim of universal
non-benevolence:

> . . . a will which resolved this
> would conflict with itself, since
> instances can often arise in which
> he would need the love and sympathy
> of others, and in which he would
> have robbed himself, by such a law
> of nature springing from his own
> will, of all hope of the aid he
> desires.[66]

It is clear that Kant thinks that human beings are so constituted that they cannot help but desire their own happiness. Indeed, for Kant, 'happiness' appears to mean nothing more than the satisfaction of inclination.[67] We might note, parenthetically, that Kant's concept of 'happiness' differs rather markedly from that of Aristotle.[68]

Given that, in Kant's view, each individual necessarily desires his or her own happiness, there is an inconsistency involved in attempting to will as a universal law any principle which would preclude the possibility of an individual's pursuing his or her own happiness. For this reason, Kant thinks that the maxim of universal non-benevolence cannot be willed as a universal law and that it is therefore morally impossible.

Has Kant really succeeded in showing the maxim of universal non-benevolence to be morally impossible? It is certainly not the case that all of the commentators on Kant's moral theory think he has succeeded. One noted commentator who does not is Robert Paul Wolff:

> Suppose an individual adopts it as his policy never to set for himself an end whose achievement appears to require the cooperation of others and to forswear any ends he has adopted as soon as it turns out that such cooperation is needed. Under these circumstances, he could consistently will that his maxim of selfishness should be a universal law of nature, for he could be certain a priori that he would never find himself willing an end which the natural law obstructed.[69]

This is surely a powerful argument and, if it is sound, Kant's position appears to be a hopeless one, because Wolff seems quite correct in his analysis of Kant's argument on this point:

138

> . . . in every situation in which
> a man finds himself, he necessarily
> wills such means as are requisite
> to his ends. That is analytically
> contained in the notion of willing
> an end. Now, *if* he ever needs the
> aid of others and *if* it should some-
> how be possible for him to determine
> the actions of those others by his
> will, then it would be inconsistent
> for him to will that they should
> not help him.[70]

The question now is, who has the better argument
on this issue, Kant or Wolff? I believe the
answer is that it is Kant.

There is one rather short-sighted counter to
Wolff's argument, and we should dispatch it immediately. One might say that, even if one agreed to
suspend pursuit of those goals which required or
appeared to require the aid of others, we would
nevertheless desire the things in question, and
thus Wolff's argument fails. This response will
not do, because it overlooks a crucial distinction
between 'willing' and mere 'wishing'. Kant writes,

> Insofar as it [the faculty of
> desire] is combined with the con-
> sciousness of the capacity of its
> action to produce its object, it
> is called *will*, or *Choice* [Willkür];
> it not so combined, its act is
> called a *wish*.[71]

Thus, for Kant, we might continue to wish for things
that were impossible for us to obtain, but we
could no longer meaningfully will them. Thus this
objection to Wolff collapses.

It seems to me that both Kant's and Wolff's
arguments are valid; that is, if their premises
are true, their conclusions must be true also.
Since the arguments reach contradictory conclusions,

it must be the case that one of the arguments has a false premise, or rests upon a false assumption. I think that it is Wolff's argument that contains this flaw.

I think that Kant would argue that we cannot know in advance which proposed ends of ours may require the assistance of others, and that we therefore cannot get around his example by setting ourselves never to desire anything which will require assistance. This is, of course, only one part of Wolff's objection. To the second part, that we would abandon any end once it became apparent that it would require assistance, one might suppose that Kant would argue that we also cannot know in advance the extent of our ability to give up ends we had set for ourselves once it becomes clear that the help of others is essential to the fulfillment of that goal. Once we have willed the universal law that no one would ever help another, we surely cannot expect to receive any aid. Thus, we could not really continue to 'will' that end, and we should have to give it up. This is the case because, as we have noted, Kant's concept of 'willing' involves one's consciousness of the capacity to do that which one wills. Thus we could not 'will', but only 'wish' for ends the fulfillment of which requires the assistance of others. Kant's position on this point reflects that of Aristotle, who writes, ". . . choice cannot relate to impossibles, and if any one said he chose them he would be thought silly; but there may be a wish even for impossibles, e.g., for immortality."[72] Thus, in this one sense, it would seem that Wolff is correct, and that one could will a policy of universal non-benevolence. But this may be only because it would become logically impossible to 'will' certain ends at all, namely, any end the achievement of which requires the assistance of others. But his is surely a technicality, and it won't do to try to overturn Kant's argument this way. Following along in this vein, one could perhaps try to show that willing a maxim of suicide was possible as a universal law since,

140

if it were universalized, it would no longer be
'suicide', but only a form of 'death by natural
causes'--and this will not do, for obvious reasons.

It also seems clear that Wolff's point is of
greater substance than this. Although Kant can
argue that our knowledge of future circumstances
is limited, so that we cannot really know in advance whether the pursuit of a particular objective will require assistance, this is not the
stronger part of Wolff's objection. To the second
part of the objection Kant cannot, despite appearances, argue that one cannot gauge in advance one's
ability to abandon objectives upon learning that
continued pursuit of them will require assistance.
If we presuppose ourselves to be free, then we
must further suppose ourselves to be capable of
rejecting any particular end, whether it requires
the aid of others or not. Surely this is required
by Kant's concept of the 'absolute spontaneity' of
the faculty of choice.

Kant cannot respond to Wolff at this point
that accepting Wolff's argument forces us to cease
being the sort of creature that we are, namely, a
being with objectives we desire to fulfill. From
the fact that we are able to relinquish any particular end, it does not follow that we are capable
of relinquishing the business of having objectives
in general. It would be an instance of the fallacy
of composition to suppose that such did follow.
Furthermore, this is hardly required for Wolff's
objection to Kant.

Is there then no rejoinder whatever that Kant
can make to Wolff's objection? I think there is
a reply open to Kant, although it surely is not
one he draws out in an explicit fashion. Suppose
one undertook to perform what one thought was a
duty. And suppose further that it turned out that,
in order to perform this duty, one would need
assistance. Here, we would have precluded not
only receiving aid in the pursuit of our desires,
but also aid in the pursuit of our duty. Or,

141

suppose that one desired to preserve one's own life, quite apart from taking it to be a duty, and that doing so on a particular occasion would require the assistance of another. In this case, abandoning the objective would constitute a violation of duty, even though duty was not the incentive of the action. In fairness to Wolff, I should note that Kant himself does not make these points.

Nevertheless, two things need to be said at this point: (1) duties are among the actions to which we may have direct inclination,[73] and thus are relevant to the present discussion; (2) these remarks are entirely consistent with Kant's general discussion of imperfect duty.

There is one further point to be made here, though it may be one that would fall prey to Wolff's objections. What I think Kant intended to say with his example of universal non-benevolence is that we ought not to treat others in ways in which we would not want to be treated (the 'golden rule' interpretation of Kant's point, we might say). And, since in general we wish to be able to pursue our goals, we ought to accord others the same privilege. It may in fact be true that we would not want other people to pass us by when we are in distress and, if this is the case, then it would be inconsistent of us to ignore the needs of others, and inconsistent for us to act in ways that would ensure that our own needs would be ignored. This would place an *a priori* limit on one's possibilities and, while this would not be inconsistent with our pursuit of any goals whatever, it does seem incompatible with the maintenance of full human possibility. I think Wolff might respond that, while limiting our goals to those that do not involve others may force us to lead a somewhat misanthropic life, it is nonetheless a life. This is true but, while it is in keeping with the letter of Kant's position, it is surely in violation of the spirit.

I think it is necessary to guard against interpreting Kant as a consequentialist at this

point. While he does speak of the consequences
of a policy of universal non-benevolence (no aid
to anyone), he does not seem to be making a pre-
diction that anyone's life plans will actually
or probably be thwarted. Rather, I take Kant to
be making the claim that it is logically possible
that such consequences arise. In order to be a
truly 'consequentialist' position, Kant would
have to be talking about actual or probable consequences, and not merely logically possible ones.

To return to the main issues here, namely,
the relation between desire and imperfect duty,
I do not think that Kant wants to argue that there
are any specific ends that all human beings necessarily desire, which then provide the basis for
imperfect duty. Indeed, if Kant did think this,
he might be able to use happiness, thus defined
in terms of those specific ends we all desire,
as a foundation for all duty,a nd he obviously
will have none of this. What Kant does seem to
want to say is that the fact that all human beings
do desire that their ends be fulfilled requires us
not to act in ways that might preclude in advance
our achieving satisfaction, or which might place
a priori limits on human possibilities.

We might conceive a world (not really so
far-fetched an assumption, this) in which all our
goals were such as to require the assistance of
others. Indeed, something like this claim is made
by the Marxists in the assertion that man is a
thoroughly social being, made what he is largely
through interactions with other human beings. It
has never been altogether clear to me what sort of
claim Marx takes this to be, but I think it may be
an empirical one, true in certain historical epochs.
If, as Marx seems to have thought, it is true in
the modern age, then Wolff's line of argument against
Kant would fail, because there would be no ends we
could will that would not require the participa-
tion of others in some way. In this case, we would
not be able to will anything at all, if we had precluded the aid of others. But his would be to

143

cease being what we essentially are, namely,
creatures with objectives wanting fulfillment.
Thus it is the general fact that we are creatures
of desire that, along with the general requirement
of universalizability (consistency), imposes imperfect duty upon it.

This last remark is important to seeing that
it is not desire alone that is the ground of obligation. Without the general requirement that our
actions be universalizable, there would be no duty
whatever, perfect or imperfect.

It may seem strange to suggest that our desires play any role whatever in determining what
our duties are. This may make Kant sound like
much too much of a utilitarian to suit some. After
all, Kant has said that ". . . all moral concepts
have their seat and origin entirely a priori in
reason . . . It is obvious that they cannot be abstracted from any empirical . . . cognitions."[74]
I think, though, that it is quite consistent for
Kant to speak of imperfect duties as he does. To
see that this is the case, it is helpful to recall
the distinction between obligation and duty. There
is a difference, I argue, between the conditions of
obligation in general and the conditions of a certain action's being a duty.

At the risk of grossly oversimplifying Kant's
view, I think we may say that freedom is the ultimate condition of obligation to the categorical
imperative in general. Kant writes, ". . . if
freedom of the will is presupposed, morality together with its principle follows from it by the
mere analysis of its concept."[75] And also,
". . . the question, 'How is a categorical imperative possible?' can be answered to this extent:
We can cite the only presupposition under which it
is alone possible. This is the Idea of freedom."[76]
Freedom, then, both in the sense of independence
of complete determination by foreign causes and in
the sense of autonomy, is the condition of obligation in general--obligation to the categorical

imperative. Freedom is, of course, a decidedly
non-empirical concept in Kant's theory.

On the other hand, the conditions under which
particular actions are duties may, and indeed
usually do, depend upon all sorts of empirical conditions. The categorical imperative, to which we
are bound if we are free, requires that we act
consistently. That is, it requires that we not
act in ways in which it would be impossible for
all other persons to act, nor in ways in which we
could not want all others to act. The requirement
that we act consistently depends on the *a priori*
condition of freedom, and on the theory of autonomous legislation, but not on our desires. But
the consistency requirement applies to our pursuit of our desires, just as well as it does to
anything else.

Thus, I think we may see how it is quite consistent for Kant to speak of imperfect duties in
the way he does. Once again, it is the distinction
between obligation and duty that enables us to see
that this is the case.

3.   Obligation and Autonomous Legislation.

Understanding Kant as being concerned with
obligation in general forces us, as I have noted,
to realize that saying that obligation applies to
all persons equally does not mean that all persons
are required to perform the same actions. Rather,
saying that obligation applies to all persons
means that all persons have duties to perform,
and that 'having a duty' or 'being under an obligation' means the same thing for all persons.

What kind of law is required for unconditional
obligation? Kant writes, ". . . duty is practical
unconditional necessity of action; it must, therefore, hold for all rational beings . . ."[77] Because persons are, by definition, rational beings,
a law valid for all rational beings will be valid
for all persons, insofar as they are rational.
But to be autonomously legislative means to be

self-legislative.[78] Thus, if there is to be the
kind of law required for unconditional obligation,
". . . it must be connected (wholly a priori) with
the concept of the will of a rational being as
such."[79] The will of a rational being is conceived by Kant as a legislative will, and it is
only when the will legislates independently of
all objects (ends) of volition, i.e., autonomously,
that the law which the will legislates will be
necessarily valid for all rational beings. Why
is the law legislated in autonomous legislation
valid for all rational beings? That is, why might
not each rational being autonomously legislate
laws valid only for himself? I should note, somewhat parenthetically, that, though the autonomously
legislated law will be valid for all rational beings,
it will be binding only on certain rational beings,
namely, those who are also free in the sense of
'absolute spontaneity'. The nature of the distinction between 'valid' and 'binding' will be made
clear later. For the moment, let it suffice to recall Kant's remarks regarding the holy will: "A
perfectly good will . . . would be equally *subject*
to objective laws . . . but it could not be conceived as *constrained* to act in accord with them,"[80]
I interpret Kant as saying that the moral law is
valid for a perfectly good will, but not binding
on it.

Let us return briefly to the question just
posed, as to why each rational being might not
autonomously legislate laws valid only for him--
or herself. Speaking of the moral law, Kant
writes,

> . . . what kind of a law can that
> be, the conception of which must
> determine the will without refer-
> ence to the expected result? . . .
> Since I have robbed the will of all
> impulses which could come to it
> from obedience to any law, nothing
> remains to serve as a principle of
> the will except universal conformity
> of its action to law as such.[81]

146

Of the principle of autonomy, Kant writes,

> Autonomy of the will is that
> property of it by which it is
> a law to itself independently
> of any property of objects of
> volition. Hence the principle
> of autonomy is: Never choose
> except in such a way that the
> maxims of the choice are com-
> prehended in the same volition
> as a universal law.[82]

Kant's point is that, to will autonomously
is to will without reference to anything one may
desire. It is to will with reference only to
one's rationality. Thus it is that Kant distinguishes autonomy from the spontaneity of the
faculty of choice. But, insofar as our rationality is concerned, all persons are exactly
alike--there is no distinguishing between
rational agents qua rational agents. Thus what
is valid for one rational being is equally valid
for all. The concept of a rational being as
such is therefore merely the logical form of
rational agency, in the same way that the transcendental unity of apperception is a logical presupposition of the possibility of empirical knowledge, rather than a concept that can be indi-
viduated and is different in different individual
knowers. As Kant says,

> The synthetic unity of consciousness
> is, therefore, an objective condition
> of all knowledge. It is not merely
> a condition that I myself require in
> knowing an object, but is a condition
> under which every intuition must stand
> in order *to be an object for me.*[83]

And, further, ". . . the judgment, 'I think' . . .
is the vehicle of all concepts . . . But it can
have no special designation, because it serves
only to introduce all our thought, as belonging
to consciousness."[84]

D.   Kant and the Tradition of Contract Theory

It will be helpful here to discuss the origins
of Kant's concept of the legislative will. Kant
is generally recognized to be a member of that tradition in social philosophy known as social contract theory. The contemporary contract theorist
John Rawls places Kant in that category.[85]   I
think one may argue that there are also elements
of contract theory in Kant's general theory of
moral obligation. I shall make some preliminary
remarks about Kant's relations to the tradition of
contract theory, and then proceed to discuss the
particular works of Hobbes, Rousseau, and Rawls,
as these writings bear on our understanding of
Kant.

Kant's position may be seen as following upon
that of Rousseau, who writes, ". . . the duty of
obedience is owed only to legitimate powers."[86]
Kant maintains that the autonomous will gives laws
valid for all rational beings, and that the autonomous will is the origin of obligation. The question arises as to why anyone ought to obey the
laws of the autonomous will. This is, of course,
a version of the question, 'Why ought I be moral?'.
Rousseau writes further that, "Since no man has
any natural authority over his fellows, and since
force alone bestows no right, all legitimate
authority among men must be based on covenants."[87]
If Kant really does take his lead from Rousseau
at this point, it would seem reasonable to think
of Kant as some sort of contract theorist. I believe that Kant does indeed follow Rousseau, and
that Kant wants to extend Rousseau's position to
include moral authority as well as legal authority.
One could be said to 'owe obedience' to the laws
of the autonomous will only if that will is a legitimate authority. The only way, for Rousseau,
that legitimate authority can be established is
through contract or 'covenant'. I should note at
this juncture that some commentators, most notably
R. P. Wolff, have cited what they take to be an
inconsistency between Kant's moral position and

his views about legal obligation. I will take up
this question in the concluding chapter, but let
me say here that I do not see in Kant the contradiction Wolff cites.

How, for Kant, is it possible for the laws
of the autonomous will to be taken as a legitimate
authority, binding on all free rational beings?
The answer to this question has two distinct
aspects: (1) there is a question about the fit-
ness or suitability of the laws of the autonomous
will (the 'general will', in Rousseau's terminology); (2) there is the question of the 'binding force' of the law of the autonomous will.
Speaking to the first question, Rousseau writes,
"how should it be that the general will is always
rightful?"[88] His answer is that,

> . . . the general will, to be truly
> what it is, must be general in its
> purposes as well as in its nature;
> that it should spring from all and
> apply to all; and that it loses its
> natural rectitude when it is di-
> rected towards any particular and
> circumscribed object for in judging
> what is foreign to us, we have no
> sound principle of equity to guide
> us.[89]

Furthermore, ". . . it cannot as a general will
give a ruling concerning any one man or any one
fact."[90] The reader will notice the strong similarities between Rousseau's remarks about the
general will and Kant's well-known position regarding the universality of the categorical imperative,
and about the necessity of abstracting from all
particular objects of inclination. Such abstracting from properties of objects of volition is,
as we have seen, the essence of Kant's concept of
autonomous legislation. The general will, or
Kant's legislative will, is potentially a legitimate authority because its dictates, by virtue of
their generality or universality, can apply equally

149

to all persons. But now there is the other side
of the question to be considered: granted for
the moment that the general or legislative will
is suitable, why is it binding? Here the concept of contract becomes illuminating. To repeat an earlier remark from Rousseau: ". . .
all legitimate authority among men must be based
on covenants."[91] I think that Rousseau would
say that the general will is binding because it
is possible for us to conceive of ourselves as
entering into a contract with our fellow persons
in which we agree to abide by the dictates of
the general will. Indeed, if we take Rousseau
seriously when he says that legitimate authority
must be based on covenant, then we must interpret him as saying that the binding force of the
general will is based on contract. I think that
this is also the most reasonable way to understand
the position Kant takes on the same point. The
categorical imperative is suitable because of its
universality, and binding because we can conceive
of ourselves as entering into a contract with our
fellow rational beings, in which we agree to abide
by the dictates of the autonomous will.[92]

There is an extremely important point to be
made here, and one which it is also fairly easy to
overlook. Just as it seems possible and appropriate to ask why one ought to consider oneself
bound by the laws of the autonomous will it appears
that I can ask why I ought to enter into a contract that would make such laws binding. I think
that Kant and, indeed, other representatives of
the tradition of contract theory, would find this
not to be an appropriate question. I shall show
why they would think this later on.

Let us review briefly what we have learned
about the autonomous (general) will, and then proceed to a more detailed analysis of Kant's relations to contract theory.[93] Several important
matters have been clarified: (1) why the autonomous will is always rightful (suitable).[94] The
autonomous will is suitable because of its universality, its applicability to all free rational

150

beings; (2) why the laws of the autonomous will are binding on all persons.[95] The laws of the autonomous will are binding on all persons because it is possible to conceive of ourselves as entering into a contract in which we agree to abide by the dictates of the autonomous will.

This last point needs some further analysis. Those who are familiar with Kant's later ethical writings are aware that Kant speaks the language of social contract theory very openly in discussing social philosophy. For example, he writes,

> . . . only the united and consenting Will of all--that is, a general united will of the people by which each decided the same for all and all decide the same for each--can legislate.[96]

The similarity of these remarks to those of Rousseau is unmistakable.

It is less obvious that Kant's theory of moral obligation, as opposed to social or legal obligation, has its roots in contract theory. Nevertheless, I do think this is the case, and I will provide some evidence for that view here.

In the early pages of the Grundlegung, Kant 'derives' the moral law from our ordinary moral experience. This 'derivation' is, of course, no mere logical 'proof', but, rather, it is what Kant calls a 'Deduction' (*Deduktion*). As John Ladd has pointed out, this is a technical term in Kant's philosophy, and should be thought of as a 'vindication' of the moral law, rather than as a strict proof of it.[97] The Deduction of the moral law from ordinary moral experience is really a regression upon the moral law as that principle in terms of which our ordinary moral judgments could make sense. The place of the moral law in the argument, then, is really as a premise rather than as a conclusion.

151

Now, so far as this part of Kant's argument
is concerned, he is certainly no contract theorist. But, the regression upon the categorical
imperative is far from being the end of the
Grundlegung. After having discussed the various
kinds of imperatives, Kant asks, ". . . how are
all these imperatives possible?"[98] He asserts
that this is a question about how the constraint
of the will involved can be conceived.[99] The question about constraint has, it seems to me, two
distinct aspects: (1) it is a metaphysical question, regarding the attributes we must suppose the
will to have in order for it to be at all possible
that we constrain ourselves to act in accord with
a categorical imperative; (2) it is also a normative question, asking for the conditions under
which a categorical imperative would be binding
or obligatory. The former aspect of the question
has been dealt with in the chapter on the 'causality' of the will. The normative dimension of
the question is at issue here. It is in regard to
this latter aspect of the question that elements
of contract theory can be seen to enter into Kant's
position.

As we saw in the chapter on the 'causality'
of the will, freedom of the will is a necessary
condition of the possibility of a categorical imperative. As we have also noted, the free will is,
for Kant, a legislative will. But legislation, as
we have further observed, is a two-term relation,
involving both a legislator or lawgiver, and a recipient of the law. That Kant thinks of legislation in this way is clear:

> A rational being belongs to the
> realm of ends as a member when he
> gives universal laws in it while
> also himself subject to these
> laws. He belongs to it as sov-
> ereign when he, as legislating,
> is subject to the will of no other.[100]

Kant, as we have seen, takes autonomous legislation to be the origin of obligation. In the case

of the state, Kant thinks that it is the idea of
contract that allows us to conceive of the authority of the state as legitimate. He writes,

> The act by means of which the
> people constitute themselves a
> state is the original contract.
> More properly, it is the Idea
> of that act that alone enables
> us to conceive of the legitimacy
> of the state.[101]

I think that we may view Kant's general theory of
moral obligation in terms of this political model.
That is, we may use the concept of a necessary and
original contract among rational beings as a vehicle for understanding Kant's theory of moral obligation. This, I think, is how Kant himself viewed
the theory of autonomy. Thus I shall be arguing
that, though freedom is clearly seen by Kant as
the 'ultimate presupposition' of the possibility
of morality, the free will is a legislative will
and the normative dimension of the theory of freedom must be understood as a contractual notion.

It may be objected that there are strong
traces of natural law theory in Kant's moral theory,
as well as elements of contract theory. While this
is no doubt true, I think that the elements of contract theory are decisive so far as Kant's theory
of obligation is concerned.

The concept of a 'realm of ends' is an important one in seeing the applicability of the contract theory model to Kant's theory of moral obligation. Kant says, "By 'realm' I understand the
systematic union of different rational beings through
common laws."[102] We are admonished to act in such
a way as to make a realm of ends possible. I interpret this to mean that we are to act as if we
were joining with our fellow rational beings in
the attempt to establish this realm of ends. It
is worth noting that the German term which has been
translated as 'realm' is *Reich*, which may equally
well be translated as 'republic', 'commonwealth',

153

or 'state'. The term itself is suggestive, therefore, of a political model of obligation. It
seems, further, that it is essentially the same
conception that one finds in such classical contract theorists as Hobbes and Rousseau, and in
such contemporaries as John Rawls. It will serve
our purposes here to consider Kant's relations to
these representatives of the tradition of contract theory in some more detail. I do not intend to give this subject as full a treatment as
it surely deserves, but it does seem important to
point out some rather strong philosophical connections between Kant's theory of autonomous legislation and the views of Hobbes, Rousseau, and the
contemporary contract theorist John Rawls. This
is not to say that there are no differences between
the views of Kant and these other thinkers, and I
shall also point out some important distinctions
as we proceed.

     There are three major topics to be discussed
here: (1) the relations between Kant's concept
of a 'realm of ends', and Hobbes' concept of a
commonwealth to be established through an 'original
contract'; (2) the similarities between Rousseau's
'general will' and Kant's concept of the Wille, or
legislative will; (3) a comparison between John
Rawl's contention that the 'original contract' ought
to be viewed as hypothetical, and Kant's reference
to a 'merely potential' realm of ends.[103] Some of
these issues have already been mentioned above,
but it will be well to elaborate upon them here.

     There is one final point to be discussed in
this section. I mentioned earlier that, while it
is appropriate to ask how we come to be bound to
the moral law, it is not equally appropriate to ask
why we ought to consider ourselves as party to a
contract among rational beings, which I think is
an important part of the answer Kant gives to the
preceding question. I shall have to show why it
is the case that the question about the contract
cannot be answered in the same manner as that about
how we can come to be bound by moral laws.

1.   Kant and Hobbes.

One might find thinking of Kant and Hobbes
in the same connection to be a case of very strange
philosophical bedfellows, indeed. Kant is, after
all, the defender of the dignity of the individual,
while Hobbes is seen as the advocate of the state's
right to deal with its citizens as it sees fit.
Both of these characterizations are somewhat
short-sighted, I think. There are some significant parallels between Kant and Hobbes on the
issue of the origins of obligation, and it is
illuminating to view Kant in terms of some of
the aspects of Hobbes' position.

My primary interest here is in Hobbes' concept of an 'original contract'. But, before turn-
ing to a discussion of this point, let us note
another aspect of Hobbes' position that bears
rather a striking resemblance to Kant's. In speaking of our obligation to the laws of nature, Hobbes
draws a distinction between obligation *in foro
externo* and *in foro interno* (literally, 'in the
external forum' and 'in the internal forum', respectively). Of this distinction, Hobbes writes,

> . . . whatsoever Lawes bind *in foro
> interno*, may be broken, not only
> by a fact contrary to the Law but
> also by a fact according to it, in
> case a man think it contrary. For
> though his Action in this case, be
> according to the Law; yet his Pur-
> pose was against the Law; which
> where the Obligation is *in foro
> interno*, is a breach.[104]

There are similarities here between Hobbe's
distinction and Kant's contrast between actions in
accord with duty, and actions from duty, though I
think we may say that Kant's position goes further
than does that of Hobbes. An action in accord
with duty would be essentially the same as an
action which, for Hobbes, was in accord with

155

obligation *in foro externo*. Kant, of course,
distinguishes between two kinds of motive that
one may have for performing an action which is
in accord with duty: the act may be done either
from duty or from inclination. In speaking of
obligations *in foro interno*, Hobbes writes, ". . .
they bind to a desire they should take place:"[105]
Hobbes does not distinguish between motives for
desiring that something take place and, indeed,
in view of his mechanistic view of human nature,
really cannot draw any such distinction. Further,
Kant would distinguish between actions which,
though they accord with duty were not what the
 agent really willed to do, and actions which
accord with duty, are what the agent willed, but
were willed for reasons other than duty. The
first of this pair might be typified by the person who attempts to cheat on his or her income
tax, multiplies incorrectly, and ends up paying
the right amount of tax by accident. The second
of the pair is one who pays taxes out of fear of
imprisonment, rather than out of a sense of obligation.

Thus there are differences between Kant and
Hobbes here, as well as similarities. I have no
wish to play down these differences, as I think
that Kant's concept of 'moral worth' is richer
than anything one can find in Hobbes. Nonetheless,
I do think that one can see in Hobbes' distinction
the germ of Kant's three-fold distinction between
actions contrary to duty, in accord with duty,
and from duty.

But now to the major point: what relations
are there between Hobbes' concept of an 'original
contract' and Kant's notion of a 'realm of ends'?
Of the need for establishing a commonwealth,
Hobbes writes,

> . . . if we could suppose a
> great multitude of men to con-
> sent to the observation of
> justice, and other lawes of

156

Nature, without a common
Power to keep them all in
awe; we might as well suppose
all Man-kind to do the same;
and then there neither would
be, nor need to be any Civill
Government, or Common-wealth
at all; because there would be
Peace without subjection.[106]

The problem of human society, as Hobbes sees it,
lies in how we are to establish this 'common
power' who will have authority over us all. I
should say, this is one of the issues with which
Hobbes is primarily concerned. Of course, he is
also interested in how such a 'common power' will
be able to enforce its regulations. On this count,
he writes,

The only way to erect such a
Common Power, . . . is, to con-
ferre all their power and
strength upon one Man, or upon
one Assembly of men. . . .[107]

Why, we may well ask, would any one want to establish such a 'common power'? Why give someone the
right and the power to force us to act in certain
ways? Hobbes' answer to this is clear: it is our
own self-preservation that moves us to transfer
our own power to the sovereign. He writes, that
each person shall ". . . owne, and acknowledge
himselfe to be Author of whatsoever he that so
beareth their Person, shall Act, or cause to be
Acted, in those things which concerne the Common
Peace and Safetie;"[108]

What of Kant's interests in these matters?
While he is doubtless interested in the enforcement of social rules (as is evident by the distinction **he** draws between internal and external
legislation), I do not think that enforcement is
Kant's primary concern in the moral sphere.
Rather, his concern here appears to be to establish

157

moral law as supreme above inclination--no reference is made to self-defense. Indeed, no such reference could be made without rendering obligation to the moral conditional, and Kant will clearly have none of this.

It is the case that both Kant and Hobbes consider it impossible that persons should live together in harmony without creating a civil authority with sufficient power to keep people under control. We have already seen something of Hobbes' views on this score. To the same point, Kant writes,

> The necessity of public lawful
> coercion does not rest on a fact,
> but on an a priori Idea of reason
> . . . because each will have his
> own right to do what seems just
> and good to him. . . . Consequently,
> the first decision that he must make,
> if he does not wish to renounce all
> concepts of justice, is to accept
> the principle that one must quit
> the state of nature . . . That is,
> before anything else, he ought to
> enter a civil society.[109]

Notice, however, that there is a great difference in the reason Kant gives for asserting that all ought to enter a civil society: it is to satisfy our sense of justice, rather than for our self-protection, as is the case with Hobbes. Despite this difference, though, Kant and Hobbes share the view that it is through contracting to be a member of a civil society that one binds oneself to the laws of a commonwealth.

To return to the question of the nature of Kant's moral theory, let us examine his concept of the 'realm of ends'. I shall argue that the model of the 'realm of ends' suggests a contract theory of obligation.

Of the 'realm of ends', Kant writes,

By 'realm' I understand the systematic union of different rational
beings through common laws. Because
laws determine ends with regard to
their universal validity, if we abstract from the personal difference
of rational beings and thus from all
content of their private ends, we
can think of a whole of all ends in
systematic connection, a whole of
rational beings as ends in themselves
as well as of the particular ends
which each may set for himself.[110]

Here, Kant asserts that a 'realm of ends' is possible only if we abstract from the private ends of
the individuals who comprise the 'realm'. What
does this mean? It is related, clearly, to what
Kant says later about the principle of autonomy:
"Autonomy of the will is that property of it by
which it is a law to itself independently of any
property of objects of volition."[111] The notion
of abstracting from private ends, however, is also
reminiscent of Hobbes' concept of each individual's
laying aside the right to decide for him- or herself how to act. Rather, the right to decide how
to act is to be 'turned over' to a central authority,
whose decisions will be binding on everyone--pre-
cisely because they have relinquished the right to
decide for themselves.

There is a significant difference between Kant
and Hobbes as well: while Hobbes is really shifting the decision-making from each individual to a
single sovereign or legislative body, who might
then proceed to choose on the basis of desires,
Kant is fundamentally shifting the criteria of decision-making from desires to principles. It will
be granted that Hobbes' sovereign decides for all,
but it is not clear that (1) the sovereign will
decide the same for all, or (2) the sovereign will
decide on the basis of some consideration other
than desire.

159

There is an important confusion to be guarded against here. It may be thought that the foregoing analysis somehow overlooks Kant's remark that each rational being belongs to this possible 'realm of ends' as both sovereign and subject, and that, therefore, each person is still to be thought of as deciding for him- or herself. Kant writes,

> A rational being belongs to the realm as a member when he gives universal laws in it while also himself subject to these laws. He belongs to it as sovereign when he, as legislating, is subject to the will of no other.[112]

It is Kant's distinction between <u>Wille</u> and <u>Willkür</u> which permits him to say, as Hobbes cannot, that the individual rational being can be both sovereign and subject in a 'realm of ends'. It is the <u>Wille</u>, as the legislative faculty of the will, which is the source of the law to which all members of the 'realm of ends' are bound, and it is the <u>Willkür</u>, as the faculty of choice, which is bound by that legislation. The legislative faculty is sovereign, the faculty of choice is subject in the 'realm of ends'. Indeed, characterizing Kant's position as involving a shifting of criteria rather than persons serves to underscore the point that, for Kant, the individual **is** to be thought of as both sovereign and subject.

It may also be objected that this analysis obscures the extreme importance of the concept of freedom of Kant's moral philosophy. But this is not the case. Rather, it is my view that this analysis places the concept of freedom in its proper perspective. It is only if the will is free, in the sense of being independent of inclination, that it could be subject to a law which abstracts from all ends posed by inclination. But being free from complete determination by inclination does not, of itself, seem to entail obligation

to anything other than inclination. This is precisely where the concept of contract becomes important to an understanding of Kant. It is
through the idea of a contract among all rational
beings (establishing a 'realm of ends') that we
are able to conceive of ourselves as bound by the
legislation of our own wills.

2. Kant and Rousseau.

The model of the contract as it appears in
Hobbes provides a vehicle for illuminating certain
things about Kant's moral theory, but not others.
For example, Hobbes' sovereign appears to have the
capacity, and perhaps even the right, to deal arbitrarily with the subjects of the commonwealth.
Dealing arbitrarily with individuals, treating them
in ways in which it is not possible or not appropriate to treat all persons, is, of course, anathema
to Kant. Kant's view of the nature of the sovereign
legislator is clearly much closer to the position
taken by Rousseau than it is to that of Hobbes. I
do think, though, that it is no great surprise that
Hobbes is willing to accord such unbridled authority to the sovereign. Hobbes is concerned about
how we are to protect ourselves from the ravages
of the state of nature, which he perceives as being
quite an unruly place, indeed.

It is clear that Rousseau is, as is Hobbes,
a contract theorist. Rousseau writes, ". . .
the social order is a sacred right which serves
as a basis for all other rights. And as it is not
a natural right, it must be one founded on covenants."[113] It is equally clear that Rousseau
views the 'original contract' as being, of necessity, a unanimous one:

> What right have the hundred who
> want to have a master to vote on
> behalf of the ten who do not? The
> law of majority-voting itself rests
> on a covenant, and implies that
> there has been on at least one
> occasion unanimity.[114]

161

It is Rousseau's concept of the 'general will' and of sovereignty that is of particular interest here. Of the sovereign, Rousseau writes, ". . . as the sovereign is formed entirely of the individuals who compose it, it has not, nor could it have, any interest contrary to theirs."[115] This begins to make clear that, for Rousseau, the sovereign cannot act arbitrarily in dealing with its subjects. But the opposite of dealing arbitrarily, of course, is dealing in ways which are valid for all. This point becomes even more clear when Rousseau discusses the 'general will'. He writes, ". . . the general will, to be truly what it is, must be general in its purpose as well as in its nature; that it should spring from all and apply to all;"[116] Thus it is clear that, for Rousseau, the general will is to be found, in some sense, in each member of the commonwealth, and its dictates apply equally to each member. Kant's concept of the 'realm of ends' echoes precisely the same sentiment:

> This legislation [making a 'realm of ends' possible], however, must be found in every rational being. It must be able to arise from his will . . . Duty pertains not to the sovereign in the realm of ends, but rather to each member, and to each in the same degree.[117]

The sense in which Rousseau's 'general will' is 'general' therefore seems to me to have been incorporated by Kant to a very significant degree.

The point about the unanimous character of the original contract has another application to Kant's theory. If I ask why I am bound to treat all persons in certain ways, e.g., as ends in themselves, we may answer that this is because it is possible to conceive of ourselves as having entered into an original contract with all other rational beings. That is, that we have a contract with each other person.

There are, of course, dissimilarities between Kant and Rousseau, just as there are between Kant and Hobbes. In this case, noting the dissimilarities is rather illuminating. There are two points of particular importance: (1) Rousseau's assertion that the general will ". . . studies only the common *interest* . . ."[118]; (2) Rousseau's contention that the dictates of the general will can be empirically calculated.[119]

In distinguishing between the 'general will' and the 'will of all', Rousseau writes,

> . . . the general will is always rightful, and always tends to the public good; but it does not follow that the decisions of the people are always equally right. We always want what is advantageous but we do not always discern it. The people is never corrupted, but it is often misled; . . . there is often a great difference between the will of all [what all individuals want] and the general will; the general will studies only the common interest while the will of all studies private interest, and is indeed no more than the sum of individual desires.[120]

The point in this with which Kant would agree, of course, is the setting aside of private interest. Kant, however, argues that we should act, ". . . independently of any property of objects of volition."[121], and not just that we should suspend personal inclination in favor of more 'publically oriented' desires. While it is not obvious whether Rousseau would accept the distinction Kant draws between acting autonomously and acting in response to some heteronomous incentive, he does say that, "We always want what is *advantageous* . . ."[122] This inclines me to think that Rousseau's position may be compatible with some forms of utilitarianism, while Kant's view is not (I say this without

163

argument here, although J.J.C. Smart has called Kant a rule-utilitarian[123]).

Rousseau and Kant also appear destined to part company on a second point: Rousseau contends, as I understand him, that the general will's dictates on any particular question may be empirically discerned. Rousseau writes,

> . . . the will of all studies private interest, and is indeed no more than the sum of individual desires. But if we take away from these same wills, the pluses and minuses which cancel each other out, the sum of the difference is the general will . . . if the general will is to be clearly expressed it is imperative that there should be no sectional associations in the state.[124]

I do not know quite what Rousseau means in speaking of this 'taking away pluses and minuses' here, but it does at least seem clear that one can, on his view, empirically discern the dictates of the general will and, by implication, one can empirically discern whether a people has acted out of its sense of obligation to the general will.[125]

It seems to me that Kant would accept neither the suggestion that the dictates of the general will can be empirically calculated, by performing some operation on the private desires of individuals, nor the associated implication that it would be possible to discern empirically whether a group of people had acted out of a sense of duty to follow the general will. To the former point, Kant writes,

> Nor could one give poorer counsel to morality than to attempt to derive it from examples. For each example of morality which is exhibited to me must itself have been

164

previously judged according to
principles of morality to see
whether it is worthy to serve as
an original example, i.e., as a
model.[126]

And, to the latter point, Kant says,

. . . if we attend to our experience of the way men act, we meet
frequent and, as we ourselves con-
fess, justified complaints that we
cannot cite a single sure example
of the disposition to act from pure
duty . . . It is in fact absolutely
impossible by experience to discern
with complete certainty a single
case in which the maxim of an action,
however much it may conform to duty,
rested solely on moral grounds and
on the conception of one's duty.[127]

Thus it appears that, despite the similarities between Kant and Rousseau regarding certain aspects
of the concept of the 'general will', Kant would
surely reject Rousseau's tendencies towards utilitarianism.

3.   Kant and Rawls.

John Rawls' recent book, A Theory of Justice[128],
is an admirable addition to the rich heritage of
social contract theory- One point of which Rawls
makes a great deal is the claim that the 'original
contract' must be viewed as merely hypothetical.
What this suggests about the function of the concept of contract is significant for an understanding of Kant's theory.

In describing the goal of his version of contract theory, Rawls writes,

My aim is to present a conception
of justice which generalizes and

165

> carries to a higher level of ab-
> straction the familiar theory of
> the social contract as found in,
> say, Locke, Rousseau, and Kant
> . . . the guiding idea is that the
> principles of justice for the basic
> structure of society are the object
> of the original agreement. They
> are the principles that free and
> rational persons . . . would accept
> in an initial position of equality
> as defining the fundamental terms
> of their association. These prin-
> ciples are to regulate all fur-
> ther agreements; they specify the
> kinds of social cooperation that
> can be entered into and the forms
> of government that can be estab-
> lished.[129]

The function of Rawls' principles of justice, in
regulating further agreements, and determining
how individuals may appropriately deal with one
another, seems to me to be an echo of Kant's views
of the categorical imperative, which has an *a
priori* regulative function in determining which
of our possible actions are morally appropriate.

Of the 'original position of equality',
Rawls says,

> This original position is not, of
> course, thought of as an actual his-
> torical state of affairs, much less
> as a primitive condition of culture.
> It is understood as a purely hypo-
> thetical situation characterized so
> as to lead to a certain conception
> of justice.[130]

And, further,

> No society can, of course, be a
> scheme of cooperation which men

166

enter voluntarily in a literal
sense; each person finds himself
placed at birth in some particular
position in some particular society,
and the nature of his position ma-
terially affects his life prospects.
Yet a society satisfying the principles of justice as fairness comes
as close as a society can to being
a voluntary scheme, for it meets
the principles which free and equal
persons would assent to under circumstances that are fair.[131]

We can ask of Rawls, as we might well ask of
Kant, why one ought to accept the principles which
would be agreed to in some merely hypothetical
situation. It is clear that the 'realm of ends'
is, for Kant, an hypothetical construct: it is,
". . . certainly only an ideal."[132] We may wonder why such hypothetical situations should be
of any interest whatever in deciding how to act.
The answer given by Rawls is that, ". . . the
conditions embodied in the description are ones
that we do in fact accept."[133] Thus the point is
that, given certain things that we do accept, it
would be inconsistent for us to refuse to accept
the principles that would be agreed to in the
original position, or, in the case of Kant, to refuse to accept the legislation of the moral law
in an hypothetical contract among rational beings.

What are some of the 'conditions of the original position' that Rawls thinks we do in fact
accept? Rawls assumes that people are essentially
self-interested, although, as he says, he does so
because he wishes to base his theory on weak
assumptions.[134] He assumes further that individuals would have, in the original position, no
specific knowledge about any special attributes
they might have that would work to their advantage
in society, nor do they have any specific knowledge
about their place in the social hierarchy, or their
family background, inherited wealth, etc.

167

Let us put Rawls' assumptions aside for the moment and see what Kant thinks we do accept that leads us to have to accept the legislation of the categorical imperative. I think that Kant believes that each person does in fact accept the hypothesis of freedom.

Kant writes, ". . . a free will and a will under moral laws are identical. Thus if freedom of the will is presupposed, morality together with its principle follows from it by the mere analysis of its concept."[135] It is thus clear what Kant thinks we are committed to if freedom of the will is presupposed. Of this presupposition, Kant says,

> We have finally reduced the definite concept of morality to the idea of freedom, but we could not prove freedom to be real in ourselves and in human nature. We saw only that we must presuppose it if we would think of a being as rational and conscious of his causality with respect to actions, that is, as endowed with a will.[136]

But it is clear, of course, that Kant believes that we do in fact think of ourselves as 'endowed with a will' and, therefore, that the obligation to the moral law is, for all practical purposes, grounded in our acceptance of freedom.

I have already alluded to the fact that there seems to be a difficulty looming on the horizon here. If it is the case that, for Kant, our acceptance of the obligation to the categorical imperative is grounded on the assumption of freedom, does it not follow that Kant has done what G. E. Moore charges: committed the 'naturalistic fallacy' by deriving an ethical judgment from a metaphysical one?[137] I do not, in fact, think that Kant has perpetrated this grievous blunder, but I shall postpone my discussion of this until the concluding chapter.

What Rawls and Kant seem to share, predominantly, is the hypothetical character of the 'original contract', which then serves as a conceptual model in terms of which obligation is made intelligible. The entire contractual framework then functions as a 'tool of criticism' against which to measure, in the case of Rawls, existing or proposed social arrangements or, in the case of Kant, possible maxims of action.

As was the case with Hobbes and Rousseau in relation to Kant, Rawls and Kant do not agree on everything. There is one particular point on which they may appear to disagree more than they actually do, however, and it is illuminating to examine this issue. The matter concerns Rawls' assumption that the individuals who are party to the 'original contract' are essentially self-interested. As Rawls says, "A conception of justice should not presuppose, then, extensive ties of natural sentiment."[138] In making this assumption, Rawls may appear to be in conflict with Kant's view that persons may be motivated by conceptions other than those of self-interest.

But I think that Kant and Rawls are in fact fairly close together here. Rawls takes this assumption for, as it were, 'strategic reasons', in order to ground his theory on the least controversial assumptions he can muster, and not because he necessarily thinks the assumption is true. For his part, Kant does indeed think that human beings are partially creatures of self-interest, and that they do and even ought to pursue their own happiness. Kant writes,

> To secure one's own happiness is
> at least indirectly a duty, for dis-
> content with one's condition under
> pressure from many cares and amid
> unsatisfied wants could easily be-
> come a great temptation to trans-
> gress duties. But without any view
> to duty all men have the strongest
> and deepest inclination to happiness,

169

because in this idea all inclinations are summed up.[139]

I think, further, that Rawls' further assumptions about the 'original position' are ideas with
which Kant would be in substantial agreement. The
lack of specific knowledge about one's position in
society, inherited wealth, skills, and the like
sound rather like a concrete way of trying to abstract from any particular properties of objects
of desire. This is, of course, how Kant characterizes autonomy. I do not think, however, that Rawls
finally adopts a theory of autonomy like the one
taken up by Kant. Rawls' analysis of human motivation is couched too much in terms of desire for
'primary social goods' to admit of direct corre-
lation with Kant's principle of autonomy.

4.   Why Enter the Contract?

It would be profitable to explore the relations between Kant's views and the whole tradition
of social contract theory in more detail, and to
analyze more fully the relations between the contractual elements within Kant's moral and social
philosophies. I think, though, that this would
take us a bit farther afield than we ought to go
here. There is one final issue that ought to be
addressed, though, before returning to a more detailed analysis of Kant's concept of the legislative will. I have said that, though it makes
sense, within a contract theory model, to ask why
one is bound to the laws of a particular commonwealth (for, say, Hobbes), or to the moral law
(for Kant), it may not make quite the same kind of
sense to ask why one ought to consider oneself as
party to such a contract in the first place. This
issue should be laid out in some detail, as it is
an important one and, also, it does not seem to
be the case that all contract theorists see this
matter in quite the same way.

Whether it makes sense to ask why we ought
to enter a contract at all depends, I think on the

170

function of the concept of contract in the particular system under consideration. Hobbes uses the notion of contract as a means of legitimizing an existing government. I do not mean by this that Hobbes' theory can justify only one specific regime, though there is little doubt that Hobbes took an interest in the justification of the British monarchy. Rather, I think Hobbes was concerned to show several things: (1) that government (virtually any government) is preferable to no government; (2) that the authority of any particular government is grounded on the concept of a contract in which we all agree to obey the laws promulgated by that particular state. For Rawls, on the other hand, the concept of the 'original contract' serves quite a different purpose: to provide a 'tool of criticism' against which to measure existing or proposed social arrangements. Thus a given society may be criticized on the grounds that it fails to provide its citizens the sorts of rights and privileges upon which they would have insisted in joining an 'original contract'.

It seems that it makes one kind of sense to ask why we ought to get ourselves involved in such a contract for Hobbes, and quite another kind of sense for Rawls. I also think that it is the case that Kant's position is more like that of Rawls than that of Hobbes, at least on this matter. I will speak to this point presently.

If we ask the question, 'Why ought I to join a contract?' of Hobbes, it is quite obvious what the answer will be: it is in our long-term self-interest to do so. Hobbes writes,

> The finall Cause, End, or Designe
> of men . . . in the introduction
> of that restraint [commonwealth]
> upon themselves . . . is the fore-
> sight of their own preservation,
> and of a more contented life
> thereby;[140]

171

Thus it is self-interest that, for Hobbes, ultimately binds us to the contract. We ought to establish a civil society, because it is in our self-interest to do so. And here, we may note, Hobbes seems to mean self-interest, rather than Hume's notion of 'true' interest. If we were to pursue the matter further, and demand to know why we ought to do that which we perceive to be in our own interest, I suspect that Hobbes would not understand the question any more than would Bentham. Bentham writes, "Nature has placed mankind under two sovereign masters, *pain* and *pleasure*."[141] Thus, if we ask 'Why ought we to do that which gives us pleasure?', Bentham would find the question incomprehensible. Hume, in like fashion, says, "If you demand, *why*? [someone desires an object] *It is the instrument of pleasure*, says he. And beyond this, it is an absurdity to ask for a reason."[142] And it is an absurdity for a very good reason, indeed: "It is impossible there can be a progress *in infinitum*, and that one thing can always be a reason why another is desired. Something must be desirable on its own account, and because of its immediate accord or agreement with human sentiment and affection."[143] For Hume as well, then, the question 'Why ought I do what is in my interest?' is devoid of sense.

But our interest here is not in the question of pleasure, but, rather, in the concept of contract. In justifying entering a contract, Hobbes will refer to pleasure, or rational self-interest. Beyond this, Hobbes will offer no justification for the pursuit of self-interest; indeed, he will find it absurd to seek such additional justification.

The situation with Rawls is, I think, rather different, although Rawls' position is so complex that I find it hard to tell exactly what his view is. If what I propose here strikes some as a perversion of Rawls' theory, it is nonetheless a coherent version of contract theory. I have said that Rawls' conception of the original contract functions as a 'tool of criticism' against which to measure, evaluate, or criticize existing or

possible institutional arrangements. This is
rather ambiguous. To make clear what is meant,
I should say that it is the contract which is
the conceptual vehicle through which we regard
ourselves as bound to certain principles which
then perform the above-mentioned critical function relative to existing or possible social
arrangements.

A question immediately arises here which
needs to be considered before proceeding any further: if the principles in terms of which we
criticize existing or possible institutions are
themselves normative (which they are, clearly,
else they would be of little use in criticism),
what need is there for reference to any further
normative device, e.g., to a contract? The
answer, I think, consists of two parts: (1) if
one is concerned only to know by what principles
to direct one's actions, then perhaps there is no
need for further normative concepts. That is, I
might accept the principle of performing only
actions that I deem valid for all persons, without considering why one ought to act in this way;
(2) from the point of view of normative theory,
the question of how we can be bound to a certain
principle or set of principles is perhaps the most
crucial issue of all. From this standpoint, reference to an 'original contract' is, for contract
theory, the decisive normative concept.

Let us return to the central matter at issue
here, which is the function of the concept of contract in Rawls' theory. I do not think that the
question 'Why ought I to consider myself as party
to a contract?' makes the same kind of sense for
Rawls that it does for Hobbes. Though it may well
be in my self-interest to join a contract, this is
not Rawls' reason for introducing the notion.
Rather, the purpose of discussing contract and the
principles of justice that would be chosen in some
'original contract' is to find principles that
would match our intuitive conception of justice.
Rawls writes,

> We can note whether applying these
> principles would lead us to make
> the same judgments about the basic
> structure of society which we now
> make intuitively and in which we
> have the greatest confidence.[144]

Of these intuitive judgments themselves, Rawls says,
"These convictions are *provisional* fixed points
which we *presume* any conception of justice must
fit."[145] I have underscored the terms 'provisional'
and 'presume' here, to highlight the fact that, for
normative theory, it is insufficient to let our
intuitions stand alone and unsupported.

Perhaps it is not yet clear why we cannot
yet ask of Rawls the same question we ask of Hobbes.
Or, rather, that we cannot expect Rawls to give
the same answer to the question: 'Why ought we
to consider ourselves party to a contract?' Rawls,
unlike Hobbes, is not attempting to justify any
particular regime, or even to account for the
existence of legitimate governments, or even to
provide reasons for establishing governments.
Rather, Rawls is trying to establish criteria
for vindicating our common-sense conceptions about
what would count as a just institution, or a fair
set of laws. He begins, then, from an intuitive
conception of justice, and regresses to the conditions under which that intuitive conception
would be binding. If we ask him why we ought to
think of ourselves as parties to a contract, he
could respond in one of two ways: (1) he could
take the 'ought' here to be a non-moral one, and
then repeat that his purpose is to 'vindicate' our
common-sense conceptions of justice; (2) he could
take the 'ought' to be genuinely normative, in
which case he would accuse his questioner of having
misunderstood what he was doing.

Could one plausibly ask whether anything in
Rawls' position is justifiable in terms of an
appeal to self-interest? I think so, but it is
not the contract itself that can be justified in
this way. Part of Rawls' concept of rationality

is the assumption that, "In choosing between principles each tries as best he can to advance his
interests."[146] Notice, however, two things about
this remark: (1) it is but one facet of Rawls'
concept of rationality, and it is decidedly not
the sole criterion for anything; (2) it is not the
contract, but, rather, the principles of justice
themselves for which self-interest is a partial
justification.

After one final word about the distinction
between Hobbes and Rawls, I shall return to Kant.
It may help to clarify the difference between
Hobbes and Rawls to say that, while they both view
the concept of contract as a normative device, designed to illustrate how we could consider ourselves as bound to certain institutions or principles, only Hobbes is willing to entertain a
normative question about the concept of contract
itself. Rawls sees the original contract as
'normatively primitive', as it were, while Hobbes
does not.

I have said that Kant's view is more like
that of Rawls than that of Hobbes. This needs
not only to be said, but also shown. To see how
Kant's view resembles Rawls' position, it is
necessary to note two things: (1) the role of
legislation in Kant's theory of obligation; (2)
the function of the concept of a 'realm of ends'
(contract) in Kant's theory. We have seen that,
for Kant, legislation is the origin of obligation.[147] It remains to consider the second question, that of the function of the concept of a
'realm of ends'. Of this concept, Kant writes,
"By 'realm' I understand the systematic union of
different rational beings through common laws."[148]
In what sense can the notion of a 'realm of ends'
be regarded as contractual? The concept of contract in classical contract theory always involves
two elements: (1) a sovereign, whose word is law
in the commonwealth resulting from the contract.
Indeed, the existence of the sovereign is itself
a product of the contract; (2) subjects who are

175

bound to the laws of the commonwealth by the act
of contracting. The role of 'subject', too, is
something that arises out of the act of contracting, and does not exist prior to it, at
least conceptually. These components are present
in Kant's analysis of the 'realm of ends'. He
writes,

> A rational being belongs to the
> realm of ends as a member when he
> gives universal laws in it while
> also himself subject to these laws.
> He belongs to it as sovereign when
> he, as legislating, is subject to
> the will of no other. The rational
> being must regard himself always as
> legislative in a realm of ends pos-
> sible through the freedom of the
> will.[149]

Just how, then, does all of this resemble Rawls'
position? There are, it seems to me, three points
of similarity, between: (1) the functions of the
'realm of ends' and Rawls' 'original position';
(2) Kant's principle of autonomy and Rawls' 'veil
of ignorance'; (3) the relation of the categorical
imperative to possible conduct and the relation
between Rawls' principles of justice and possible
or existing social arrangements.

For Rawls, as we have seen, we can imagine
certain principles of justice to be binding if we
can imagine them to be the ones that would be
chosen in the 'original position'. Thus, the concept of the 'original position' and of agreements
reached from that vantage-point serve to vindicate our intuitive sense of justice, and to show
how we can imagine ourselves bound to principles
of justice. For Kant, I think the concept of a
'realm of ends' is the conceptual vehicles through
which we conceive of ourselves as bound to the
moral law. This serves as a vital link in the
vindication of our commonsense moral intuitions.
Without the concept of a 'realm of ends', we could

see only that the categorical imperative accords with our intuitions about duty and obligation, but we could not see how we could imagine ourselves as bound to it.

It may be objected here that this analysis, once again, obscures the role of the concept of freedom in Kant's moral theory. Again, I do not think that this is the case, and I shall argue for this view in the concluding chapter.

The various 'suspensions of knowledge' that Rawls imposes on us through his 'veil of ignorance' is, as already noted, much like the abstraction from properties of objects of volition that characterizes Kant's concept of autonomy.[150] The importance of this point is that it, too, serves as a presupposition required to vindicate our common-sense conceptions of justice or morality, rather than being principles from which particular judgments are derived.

Finally, there is a correspondence between Kant's and Rawls' view of the function of the principles that would be selected from the 'original position'. Both Kant's categorical imperative (the principle which, for Kant, would govern a 'realm of ends'), and Rawls' two principles of justice serve what we may call a 'regulative' function in relation to conduct or to possible or existing institutional arrangements. These principles are criteria against which possible actions (in the case of Kant) and possible or existing institutions are to be evaluated.

Kant does not so far as I can tell, treat the concept of contract in the same way Hobbes does, although Kant does argue, as vehemently as does Hobbes, that persons must establish civil society. Kant writes,

> . . . the first decision that he
> must make, if he does not wish to
> renounce all concepts of justice,

177

> is to accept the principle that one
> must quite the state of nature, in
> which everyone follows his own
> judgment, and must united with
> everyone else . . . That is, before
> anything else, he ought to enter a
> civil society.[151]

Notice, though, that Kant's reason for saying one
ought to enter a civil society is quite different
from that given by Hobbes. For Hobbes the reason
is self-preservation and contentment[152], while
for Kant the reason is the vindication of our concept of justice.[153] Thus I think that the concept
of contract in social philosophy performs for Kant
a function similar to that performed by the 'realm
of ends' in his moral theory. Indeed, I believe
that they are essentially the same notion in different connections.

Duties of justice are, for Kant, duties which
can be legislated externally, and, "A state
(*civitas*) is a union of a multitude of men under
laws of justice."[154] There is an obvious parallel
between this and Kant's remark about the 'realm of
ends': "By 'realm' I understand the systematic
union of different rational beings through common
laws."[155]

E. Autonomy and Legislation.

One crucial issue that has not yet been discussed adequately is the following: how is it that
the autonomous will is a legislative will? The requirement that the autonomous will be a legislative
will seems to follow upon several premises: (1)
legislation is the origin of obligation; (2) legislation contains the concept of law;[156] (3) the
kind of law required for moral obligation can originate only in an autonomous will. The law must be
legislated, handed down, as it were, before it can
be said that there is obligation to the law. The
law must be legislated by the same autonomous will
which is the origin of the law. If the autonomous

178

will which is the origin of the law were not the
legislative faculty, then, since the law would
have to be legislated by some other faculty, the
unconditional nature of the imperative would be
lost. This last point rests upon Kant's contention in the Grundlegung that all sources of law
and legislation beyond one's own will are heteronomous, and, therefore, conditional.[157]

I have already noted that legislation is a
two-party relationship. Let us now examine this
contention in more detail. Legislation involves
a legislator, or one who binds, and a 'recipient', or one who is bound.[158] The autonomous will
is the legislator, in this instance. Who or what
is bound by the legislation of the autonomous
will? The answer seems clear, though somewhat
paradoxical: one must bind oneself in autonomous
legislation. This must be the case, given that
'autonomy' is derived from the Greek terms *auto*
(self) and *nomos* (law). But how can this be?
What sense does it make to say that one binds oneself?[159] It is, of course, intelligible to speak
of one person binding another. Hobbes' sovereign
binds persons to perform certain actions. It
might well turn out that these actions are not performed, were they not so required. The idea here
is that of someone in authority requiring that others
perform certain actions. But the autonomous will
is always rightful, and cannot err. So, what sense
does it make to speak of the autonomous will as
being bound, since by its very nature it cannot
err? Indeed, it is misleading to speak of the
autonomous will as acting at all, since it is concerned, not with action, but with legislation for
the maxims of actions.[160]

In fact, it does not make sense to speak of
the autonomous will as bound or obligated, and it
is not the autonomous will that Kant asserts to
be obligated by the categorical imperative.[161]
But, then, the question arises again, who or what
is bound by the legislation of the autonomous will?
To answer this question, we shall have to return

179

once more to the distinction between two senses of 'will'.

What we will discover, I think, is that there is an important ambiguity in Kant's use of the notion of 'autonomy'. Sometimes the notion seems to refer to the legislative faculty alone, and at other times to the combined faculty. I think that the concept of autonomy most properly applies to the combined faculty, rather than to <u>Wille</u> alone.

F.   The Relation Between Kant's Concept of
      Legislation and the Concept of the Free Will.

It is important to note at this juncture that a distinction between the autonomous will and the faculty of choice is necessary if sense is to be made of the kind of legislation required for moral obligation. Kant makes this distinction in terms of the by now familiar two senses of 'will'. If the one who binds is identical to the one who is bound, then there could be no obligation at all, because one could always release oneself from the obligation. As Kant says,

> If the 'I' who obligates is taken
> in the same sense as the 'I' who is
> obligated, then the concept of duty
> to oneself is self-contradictory
> . . . This contradiction can also be
> brought to light by pointing out that
> the one who binds (*auctor obligationis*)
> could always release the one bound
> (*subjectum obligationis*) from the
> obligation (*terminum obligationis*).[162]

If the will that is the origin of the categorical imperative were taken in the same sense as the will that is bound by the imperative, then, in so far as choice is the essence of one sense of will,[163] one could choose whether or not to be bound by the categorical imperative. Though one may, and indeed must be able to, choose whether or not to respond to the categorical imperative, Kant would consider it quite absurd to say that one could choose

180

whether or not to be obligated by the categorical imperative. Saying this would make the obligation to the categorical imperative conditional, and this would quite obviously conflict with the central thesis of Kant's position.

Kant seems to want to resolve this problem, as he does other apparent difficulties with his practical philosophy, through a recourse to the 'doctrine of two standpoints'. He writes,

> Man regards himself, in his consciousness of a duty to himself, as being the subject of it in a double sense: first, as a sensible being [*Sinnenwesen*], i.e., as a man . . . but, then, also as an intelligence [*Vernunftswesen*] (not merely as a being possessing reason [*vernunftiges Wesen*], . . . [164]

I think, as I have already suggested, that the 'doctrine of two standpoints' is limited in the extent to which it can be employed to account for obligation. That is, the theory of freedom, in the sense of independence from complete determination through inclination, only explains how the normative force of the moral law can be applied to us as finite human beings; it does not, so far as I can see, account for that normative force itself. Here, as elsewhere, I find the contract model of obligation illuminating.

[1] FMM, p. 439.

[2] Ibid., p. 446. This sense of negative freedom is not to be confused with political liberty.

[3] Critique II, p. 31.

[4] There is no question but that Wille will legislate because, for Kant, reason must be 'intrinsically practical' (Cf., Lewis White Beck, A Commentary on Kant's Critique of Practical Reason, p. 41). It should be noted that the way Kant links freedom with obligation appears to be, on the surface at least, a rather radical view. That is, one might normally think that obligation implies freedom, that it makes no sense to speak of one's being obligated unless one is free to either perform the obligation or not. Kant's view includes this, but also includes the reverse: if one is free, then one is obligated to the moral law; that is, obligation also presupposes freedom.

[5] FMM, p. 439.

[6] Lewis White Beck, A Commentary on Kant's Critique of Practical Reason, p. 41.

[7] Justice, p. 227.

[8] FMM, p. 412.

[9] Ibid., pp. 445-46.

[10] Strictly speaking, the response is not in one's actions, but in the choice of one's maxims for action. The effect of which the Wille is a cause, (only a partial cause, at most) is the adoption of a morally appropriate maxim. I believe this is correct though, as we have noted, it must be possible in principle for the choices we make to have an impact on the phenomenal realm.

This is clear from the analysis of the Third
Antinomy.

[11]FMM, p. 416.

[12]Ibid., p. 413.

[13]The term 'autonomy' is derived from the
Greek *auto*, meaning 'self', and *nomos*, meaning
'law'.

[14]Religion, p. 40.

[15]FMM, p. 439.

[16]Ibid., p. 427.

[17]Cf., Justice, p. 218. It should be noted
that, for Kant, obligation contains, ". . . not
only practical necessity (of the sort that a law
in general asserts), but also constraint," (Ibid.,
p. 223). This accords quite naturally with the
two elements in legislation, law and incentive.
Practical necessity is contained in the law, and
constraint in the incentive. I interpret the remark that law makes actions duties as meaning that
the law sets formal limits for actions. It does
not, and indeed cannot, mean that all particular
duties are entailed by the law alone.

[18]Ibid., p. 219.

[19]FMM, pp. 397-98.

[20]Justice, p. 219.

[21]I say 'may be' here, because the incentive
must be freely chosen; so long as an action is a
duty, the internal incentive is a possible incentive.

[22]Cf., R. P. Wolff, In Defense of Anarchism.

[23]FMM, p. 439.

[24]Justice, p. 222.

[25] Kant, _Virtue_, pp. 417-18.

[26] _Ibid_.

[27] Cf., _FMM_, pp. 397-98.

[28] _Ibid_., p. 397.

[29] _Justice_, p. 220, my emphasis.

[30] _Ibid_.

[31] Later remarks will serve to clarify Kant's concept of freedom. The reader may also refer to the previous chapter on the 'causality' of the will.

[32] _FMM_, p. 414.

[33] Lewis White Beck, _A Commentary on Kant's Critique of Practical Reason_, p. 41.

[34] Jeremy Bentham, _Op.cit._, Chap. III.

[35] _Ibid_.

[36] _Ibid_.

[37] _Ibid_.

[38] _Ibid_.

[39] _Ibid_.

[40] _Ibid_.

[41] David Hume, _Inquiry Concerning the Principles of Morals_, was first published in 1752; Bentham's _Principles_ was first printed in 1780, and first published in 1789.

[42] Hume, _Inquiry_, p. 47, my emphasis.

[43] _Ibid_., p. 99.

[44]Ibid., p. 100.

[45]FMM, p. 449.

[46]Ibid., p. 450, my emphasis.

[47]J. S. Mill, Utilitarianism, Chap. III.

[48]Cf., G. E. Moore, Principia Ethica, Chap. 2.

[49]Mill, Op.cit., Chap. III.

[50]Ibid.

[51]Ibid.

[52]Hume, Inquiry, p. 99.

[53]Ibid., p. 100.

[54]Mill, Op.cit., Chap. III.

[55]Justice, p. 227.

[56]Cf., FMM, p. 439; Justice, p. 227.

[57]Justice, p. 222.

[58]FMM, p. 425.

[59]Ibid., p. 440.

[60]'Legislation' is the translation, once again, of the German term *Gesetzgebung*, meaning a 'giving of law'.

[61]By 'independently of objects of volition' and 'without reference to inclination' here, I mean that obligation cannot be established upon a foundation of inclination, that inclination cannot serve as the supreme principle of morality. I do not mean, nor does Kant, that it is never morally appropriate, perhaps even obligatory to satisfy an inclination. Kant is certainly no ascetic.

[62] This seems to be the thrust of Section III of _FMM_.

[63] Cf., _FMM_, pp. 421-24.

[64] Cf., Gary M. Hochberg, "A Re-examination of the Contradictions in Kant's Examples", _Philosophical Studies_, 1973; "The Concept of 'Possible Worlds' and Kant's Distinction Between Perfect and Imperfect Duties", _Philosophical Studies_, 1974.

[65] _FMM_, p. 424.

[66] _FMM_, p. 423.

[67] _Ibid._, p. 399.

[68] Cf., Aristotle, _Nicomachean Ethics_.

[69] R. P. Wolff, _The Autonomy of Reason_, pp. 170-71.

[70] _Ibid._, p. 170.

[71] _Justice_, p. 213.

[72] Aristotle, _Nicomachean Ethics_, Bk. III, Ch. 2.

[73] Cf., _FMM_, pp. 397-98.

[74] _Ibid._, p. 411.

[75] _Ibid._, p. 447.

[76] _Ibid._, p. 461.

[77] Kant's distinction between perfect and imperfect duties is relevant here. Imperfect duties (e.g., benevolence) do depend in part upon inclination. That is, they depend upon our having a subjective constitution which is such that we necessarily desire our own happiness. But, though desire is thus required for the existence of imperfect duty, desire is not the ultimate condition

upon which the possibility of all duty whatever is founded.

[78]FMM, p. 425.

[79]Ibid., p. 440.

[80]Ibid., pp. 413-14, my emphasis.

[81]Ibid., pp. 401-02.

[82]FMM, p. 440.

[83]Critique I, p. B138.

[84]Ibid., pp. A341, B399-400.

[85]Cf., John Rawls, A Theory of Justice.

[86]FMM, p. 426.

[87]Jean-Jacques Rousseau, The Social Contract, p. 53.

[88]Ibid.

[89]Ibid., p. 75.

[90]Ibid.

[91]Ibid., p. 77.

[92]Ibid., p. 53.

[93]Cf., Gary M. Hochberg, "Why Kant's Categorical Imperative is Binding" (unpublished).

[94]It should not be thought that there are no differences whatever between Kant and Rousseau. Rousseau takes it that the 'general will' can be determined in particular cases, and for particular actions--though it can never be used for particular advantage. It is not clear to me that Kant's autonomous will can be said to be directly

187

legislative for all particular cases. In the
case of Kant, it seems to me to make more sense
to think that the autonomous will, in legislating the moral law, legislates a formal constraint
upon the human will, but that this does not entail the legislation of specific particular
actions in all cases. For a more detailed discussion of Kant and Rousseau, see "Collective
Decision-Making in Rousseau, Kant, Hegel, and
Mill", by C. Dyke (_Ethics_, Vol. 80, No. 1, 1969).

[95]The observation that the autonomous will
cannot err is relevant to the possibility of
there being a law making actions duties. It is
extremely difficult to make the notion of a 'completely rational will' intelligible. The idea
seems to be that the autonomous will contains
nothing empirical, nothing that refers to inclination or desire. It is a purely formal will,
and a completely rational legislation is one which
is binding for the formal characteristics of
actions.

[96]_Justice_, pp. 313-14.

[97]Cf., John Ladd, translator's introduction to
Kant's _Justice_, p. xxvii.

[98]_FMM_, p. 417.

[99]_Ibid_.

[100]_Ibid_., pp. 433-34.

[101]_Justice_, p. 315.

[102]_FMM_, p. 433.

[103]_Ibid_., p. 439.

[104]Hobbes, _Leviathan_, ed. by C. B. MacPherson,
p. 215.

[105]Hobbes, _Op.cit_., p. 215.

[106] _Ibid._, p. 225.

[107] _Ibid._, p. 227.

[108] _Ibid._, my emphasis.

[109] _Justice_, p. 312.

[110] _FMM_, p. 433.

[111] _Ibid._, p. 440.

[112] _Ibid._, pp. 433-34.

[113] Jean-Jacques Rousseau, _Op.cit._, p. 50.

[114] _Ibid._, p. 59.

[115] _Ibid._, p. 63.

[116] _Ibid._, p. 75.

[117] _FMM_, p. 434.

[118] Rousseau, _Op.cit._, p. 72, my emphasis.

[119] _Ibid._, pp. 72-73.

[120] _Ibid._, p. 72.

[121] _FMM_, p. 440.

[122] Rousseau, _Op.cit._, p. 72, my emphasis.

[123] Cf., J. J. C. Smart, "An Outline of a System of Utilitarian Ethics," in _Utilitarianism: For and Against_, by Smart and Bernard Williams.

[124] Rousseau, _Op.cit._, pp. 72-73.

[125] L. G. Crocker, _Rousseau's Social Contract_, pp. 69-70.

[126] _FMM_, p. 408.

[127] FMM, pp. 406-07.

[128] John Rawls, A Theory of Justice (Harvard: 1971).

[129] Ibid., p. 11.

[130] Ibid., p. 12.

[131] Ibid., p. 13.

[132] FMM, p. 433.

[133] Rawls, Op.cit., p. 21.

[134] Ibid., p. 129.

[135] FMM, p. 447.

[136] Ibid., pp. 448-49.

[137] Cf., G. E. Moore, Principia Ethica, Chap. 4.

[138] Rawls, Op.cit., p. 129.

[139] FMM, p. 399.

[140] Hobbes, Op.cit., p. 223.

[141] Bentham, Op.cit., Chap. I.

[142] Hume, Inquiry, p. 111.

[143] Ibid.

[144] Rawls, Op.cit., p. 19.

[145] Ibid., p. 20, my emphasis.

[146] Ibid., p. 142.

[147] Cf., Justice, p. 227.

[148] FMM, p. 433.

[149] Ibid., pp. 433-34.

[150] Cf., Rawls, Op.cit., pp. 136-42; FMM, p. 440.

[151] Justice, p. 312.

[152] Cf., Hobbes, Op.cit., p. 223.

[153] Justice, p. 312.

[154] Ibid., p. 313.

[155] FMM, p. 433.

[156] It is extremely important for Kant's moral theory that the autonomous will be binding in this way: binding on one only because it is binding on all. In order for legislation (of the categorical imperative) to be binding in this fashion, it must be legislated autonomously, independently of anything that individuals happen to desire. If the categorical imperative were not autonomously legislated, there would be no guarantee that the imperative would be binding on all persons.

[157] Legislation 'contains' law: I take this to mean that the concept of the act of legislation includes that of law; that it makes no sense to speak of legislation without making reference to a law that is legislated.

[158] Cf., FMM, p. 444.

[159] Cf., Virtue, p. 417.

[160] Cf., Gary M. Hochberg, "Why Kant's Categorical Imperative is Binding", (unpublished).

[161] Cf., Justice, p. 226.

[162] Cf., Ibid., p. 213.

163_Virtue_, p. 417.

164_Ibid_., p. 418.

Chapter IV: Concluding Remarks and Lingering
            Difficulties.

    There are many matters I would like to
address by way of conclusion, and I will likely
satisfy no one in the process. Nonetheless, it
seems important to attempt to speak to a range
of issues that remain, including: the relation
of Kant's theory of legislation to his general
moral theory as that is sketched out in the
Grundlegung; some lingering difficulties with the
distinction between Wille and Willkür; some difficulties with the contract theory interpretation of Kant's theory of obligation. This latter
point is especially important since there are un-
doubtedly those who, if they have read this far
at all, have grave reservations about the emphasis on legislation and contract theory in an
analysis of Kant's theory of obligation. It is
probably not possible to persuade everyone about
these matters, but I do sense an obligation to try.

A. An Analysis of the Central Questions of the
    Grundlegung in Terms of the Concept of Moral
    Legislation.

    The results of our discussions of the concept
of legislation may be related to the central questions of Kant's Grundlegung. It will be well to
draw out this relation to the Grundlegung here,
because it serves to tie together the concept of
legislation and Kant's overall theory of moral
obligation. I consider the following to be the
three central questions of the Grundlegung: (1)
how can there be obligation of the sort of which
we seem to be aware in our ordinary moral experience; (2) how is a categorical imperative
possible; (3) how can reason be practical? I
think it is possible to understand these three
questions in terms of Kant's concept of moral
legislation.

    Kant's answer to the first question, how there

can be obligation of the sort of which we are
aware in ordinary moral experience, is that obligation is possible only if a categorical imperative is possible. He purports to show this in
illustrating why morality cannot be derived from
examples.[1] It is in his discussion of the second
question, how a categorical imperative is possible, that we may begin to weave the concept of
legislation into the picture.

What is a categorical imperative? In answering this, it will be helpful to recall Kant's remarks regarding imperatives in general. Kant
writes, "The conception of an objective principle
so far as it constrains a will, is a command (of
reason), and the formula of this command is called
an imperative."[2] The central concept underlying
the notion of an imperative is thus that of constraint. Constraint, as we have already noted,
means that an action is made 'practically necessary', or that the action is presented as being
one which ought to be done. Actions which are
thus presented are divided by Kant into the two
by now notorious classes of actions good as means
to some subjective purpose (hypothetical imperatives) and actions good in themselves (duties, or
actions required by a categorical imperative). A
categorical imperative is thus a law which commands or prescribes, and not a law which merely
describes the way actions of a certain sort occur,
as is the case with, for example, scientific laws.

But how else can such binding laws arise
except through legislation? Asking how a categorical imperative is possible, then, is to ask
how it is possible for binding laws to be given.
Once again, we should recall what Kant says at the
close of his discussion of imperatives:

> . . . how are all these impera-
> tives possible? This question
> does not require an answer as to
> how the action . . . can be per-
> formed but merely as to how the

constraint of the will . . .
can be conceived.[3]

And, further, "To see how the imperative of morality is possible is, then, without doubt the only
question needing an answer."[4] Thus we can see,
first, that Kant considers the question of the
possibility of the categorical imperative's being
an imperative (being binding) to be a question in
need of an answer, and, second, that the focal
point of this question is the notion of constraint.
We have already seen how the concept of legislation relates to constraint.

In answering the question, how a categorical imperative is possible, Kant asserts that
such an imperative is possible only if reason
can be practical. By 'practical', Kant means
that reason can, independently of objects of volition, establish the goals of action.[5] Establishing the goals or ends of action is legislation. And an establishing of goals independently
of any objects of volition is autonomous legislation.

Ultimately, then, asking how reason can be
'practical' is to ask how autonomous legislation
is possible. Kant ultimately regresses upon freedom as the ultimate presupposition of the possibility of autonomous legislation.[6]

B.   Problems with the Wille/Willkür Distinction
      and with the Concept of Autonomy.

Three issues arise from Kant's distinction
between the two senses of 'will' and particularly
with the concept of autonomy: (1) what is the
precise role of the concept of autonomy in the
origin of obligation; (2) why are all autonomous
rational beings necessarily bound by the same
moral law; (3) why must moral obligation be the
result of autonomous legislation?

195

1.   Autonomy and the <u>Wille/Willkür</u> Distinction.

It seems most plausible to say that it is
the entire rational faculty of the will which is
autonomous, rather than that one aspect of the
will or the other is autonomous. Why is this
interpretation correct?

Autonomy is, ". . . the property of the will
to be a law to itself."[7] Kant formulates the distinction between the two senses of 'will' because
he thinks that morality is possible only if the
will can be a law to itself and because he thinks
that the idea of the will's thus being a law to
itself, without such a distinction, is logically
absurd. The distinction thus has logical rather
than ontological status. As Kant writes,

> If the 'I' who obligates is taken
> in the same sense as the 'I' who
> is obligated, then the concept of
> a duty to oneself is self-con-
> tradictory . . . Therefore, if
> both are one and the same subject,
> then he would not be bound at all
> by a duty he imposes on himself,
> and this involves a contradiction.[8]

What is autonomous here is a giving of law
(*Gesetzgebung*). A giving of law is not something
that occurs, as it were, in a vacuum. Law-giving
cannot occur without a potential recipient. To
put the matter in yet another way, law-giving, or
legislation, is always a two-term relation. Legislation is, in Kant's philosophy, an activity, or
process.[9] It is of great importance for an understanding of Kant's position that his concept of
legislation not be confused with statutes which
would have to be understood, in Kant's terms, as
the results of legislation.

It may seem a bit peculiar that the faculty
of choice, which is generally thought of as being
negatively free, is an integral component in the

autonomous will (where autonomy is taken as being positive freedom, the capacity of being a law to oneself). But, indeed, this has to be the case. There can be no command without both one who commands and one who is commanded. And, further, there can be no law-giving without the implicit acceptance on the part of the recipient of the legislation. Thus, when Kant speaks of the autonomous will, he must be understood as speaking of the combined faculty which includes both <u>Wille</u> and <u>Willkür</u>. It should also be said here that, while all acts of legislation imply at least tacit acceptance, the reverse is not true: the will might assent to some principle which was not objectively valid, i.e., could not apply to all persons, and which therefore could not be a law.

It is perhaps clear enough that positive freedom (autonomy) involves negative freedom (spontaneity), in the sense that autonomous law-giving requires a negatively free recipient. How is it, though, that negative freedom requires or involves positive freedom? Negative freedom, to be 'freedom' in a strong sense of that term, requires that it be possible to select from among a range of significantly different alternatives. If one's alternatives all come down to the satisfying of some sort of inclination, then, in a sense, all one's alternatives are of the same kind. Pleasure is, in the final analysis, pleasure, and pushpin is as good as poetry, though there may of course be long-term and short-term pleasures between which we may distinguish. One is negatively free, in a situation in which all of one's alternatives involve service to inclination, only to the extent that one can decide which inclination to satisfy. The addition of positive freedom to the picture, however, gives one something more than just a range of alternatives all of which are of the same sort. Positive freedom, or autonomy, is a property of the will, ". . . by which it is a law to itself independently of any property of objects of volition."[10] Such choices would be alternatives of a sort that is radically different from the

197

alternatives of satisfying one inclination or
another. Negative freedom in the strongest sense
requires these 'significantly different' alternatives and, hence, requires positive freedom.
This will serve to illustrate the claim I made
much earlier that one cannot really make much
sense of Kant's notions of either positive or
negative freedom without talking about the other.
The two conceptions are reciprocal.

Let us consider briefly an objection to Kant's
position here. One can imagine, say, John Stuart
Mill, charging that the notion of being motivated
to act independently of any object of volition
whatever is absurd. The second part of the 'proof'
of the principle of utility, in Mill's Utilitarianism,
is, of course, designed to show that one never desires anything other than happiness and that, therefore, it is the only thing that is desirable, in
the normative sense of that term. Although this
is scarcely the place to enter upon a lengthy discussion of Mill's views, we may say briefly that
Kant would likely respond that Mill has begged precisely the question that he most needs to answer.
That is, given what Kant takes to be the nature of
our ordinary moral experience, we take it to be
obligatory, at least on occasion, to do things
other than those we want to do. It will not do for
Mill to claim, without argument, that we can have
no source of motivation other than desire, since
the possibility of such other motivation is precisely what is at issue. Indeed, I am not certain
that Mill does actually *assume* this empirical
theory of human motivation, though I do think it
is clear that his utilitarian forebears Bentham
and Hume make such an assumption.

I think it is correct to term autonomy a property of the entire rational faculty of the will,
although there is some disagreement about this in
the secondary literature. In Kant: The Philosophy
of Right, Jeffrie Murphy writes,

> Kant uses the phrase 'free will'
> or simply 'freedom' quite

> ambiguously. Though he has two
> technical meanings of freewill,
> he usually fails to keep them
> separate. His technical uses
> are as follows: . . . Free
> Willkür: Freedom of choice or
> the spontaneous self-activity of
> persons . . . Free Wille:
> Autonomy or acting on the basis
> of a universal law of reason.[11]

Though the point of Murphy's discussion is to argue
that Willkür rather than Wille must be the ground
of dignity[12], I think we may see an error here in
his treatment of the concept of autonomy itself.
Kant calls autonomy of the will the, ". . . property of it by which it is a law to itself independently of any property of objects of volition."
Now, unless we are to think that Kant means that
Wille is a law to Wille, we cannot think of
autonomy as being a property of Wille alone.
Even if it made sense to speak of Wille's being
a law to Wille, this would not solve the problem
of binding Willkür to the law. In fact, it does
not make any sense to speak of Wille's being a law
to Wille since Wille legislates, not for itself,
but for maxims of action - action, of course, is
a function of the faculty of choice, and not of the
legislative faculty.

Perhaps another way of putting this objection
to Murphy's analysis is to observe that the references to autonomy in the Grundlegung are to the
combined faculty of the will. That is, as we have
already noted, Kant draws no systematic distinction
between Wille and Willkür in the Grundlegung and
generally refers to the combined faculty of the
will when he uses the term Wille. This is certainly
true of the references to autonomy. Perhaps more
telling, I know of no place where Kant uses the
notion of autonomy in connection with Wille while
maintaining a systematic distinction between the
two senses of 'will'.

I also think that Murphy's suggestion that it is the spontaneity of Willkür that yields the dignity of the person is at least misleading. What Kant actually says on this score is that,

> . . . morality is the condition under which alone a rational being can be an end in itself, because only through it is it possible to be a legislative member in the realm of ends. Thus morality and humanity, so far as it is capable of morality, alone have dignity.[14]

Further, Kant says, "Morality . . . consists in the relation of every action to that *legislation* through which alone a realm of ends is possible."[15] Since legislation is obviously required for morality, and the capacity for morality is the ground of the dignity of persons, it seems to follow that legislation (which is, of course, a function of Wille), is at least an integral component in human dignity. To be sure, the spontaneity of the faculty of choice is *also* required, but this merely serves to illustrate that spontaneity and legislation are reciprocal concepts.

2.   Why There is But One Moral Law.

What is the precise role of the legislative faculty in the origin of obligation? The answer, quite simply, is that Wille is the source of the law to which one is bound. Does this not commit us to saying that, on Kant's view, the law of which the legislative faculty is author is arbitrary?[16] Kant says,

> He who commands (*imperans*) through a law is the *lawgiver* (legislator). He is the originator (*auctor*) of the obligation imposed by the law, but is not always the originator of the law. If he is, then the law is contingent (positive) and arbitrary.[17]

This passage seems to be in conflict with the following passage from the Grundlegung:

> The will is thus not only subject to the law but subject in such a way that it must be regarded as self-legislative and only for this reason as being subject to the law (of which it can regard itself as author).[18]

I think that these two passages are compatible if interpreted in the following way: the law which reason formulates of itself must be a law of a certain sort, and it is therefore necessary rather than arbitrary. Thus it is possible for Kant to say that one's reason is the author of a moral law without this thereby meaning that the law is arbitrary. Put another way, it may be a contingent matter whether there are any rational beings who are free in the specific sense required for obligation, but, if there are any such free rational beings, they are necessarily bound by the moral law.

The resolution of this last difficulty answers the question: why must all autonomous rational beings be subject to the same law? The first point that Kant has in mind here is that this is a law such that one is subject to it only because it is a law for all persons, in the sense that the categorical imperative is a formal constraint on the maxims of the will.[19] Secondly, the law is to be a law formulated without reference to, as Kant says, ". . . any property of objects of volition."[20] The point here is that all persons are alike, when considered solely as free rational agents.[21] A law formulated from such a point of view, namely, without reference to inclination, would necessarily be the same for all persons. That is, the law (the categorical imperative) is a necessary product of the will of a rational being as such, and, thus, any rational being's will must produce the same law.[22]

201

3.   Morality and Autonomous Legislation.

Why must the moral law be the product of
autonomous legislation, rather than being hetero-
nomously derived?[23]   In a sense, Kant is asking
a version of the question 'Why should I be moral?'
in insisting that the moral law must be autonomously legislated. If one is bound by the desire
for happiness, it still seems to make sense to
ask whether one ought to do what will contribute
to one's happiness. Or, if one takes oneself to
be bound by the will of God, the question 'Why
should I do what God commands?' remains a legitimate question. If, on the other hand, one is
bound by one's own will (as is the case with
autonomous legislation), it does not make the same
kind of sense to ask 'Why should I do that which
I have bound (obligated) myself to do?' It makes
perfectly good sense to ask why I bound myself to
a certain course of action, or whether a certain
course of action is something to which I should
have bound myself, but these are questions of a
different sort. The only kind of problem that
can arise in the present context concerns why one
ought to be bound by the kind of law which arises
out of autonomous legislation, and we have already seen how Kant deals with that sort of
question.

4.   The 'Abridgement' of Spontaneity.

There is a final point in Jeffrie Murphy's
analysis of freedom and autonomy which ought to be
addressed before we move on to other matters.
Murphy notes that, though on his interpretation
of Kant it is the freedom of Willkür that yields
dignity, it surely cannot be the case that Kant
would have us stand idly by and, to take Murphy's
own example, witness a rape.[24] What is needed,
obviously, is some theory of what I will call
the 'legitimate abridgement of spontaneity'. On
the question of 'hindrances to freedom', Kant writes,

> Any opposition that counteracts the
> hindrance of an effect promotes that

> effect and is consistent with it
> . . . everything that is unjust is
> a hindrance to freedom . . . Coer-
> cion, however, is a hindrance or
> opposition to freedom. Consequently,
> if a certain use of freedom is it-
> self a hindrance to freedom *accord-*
> *ing to universal laws* . . . then the
> use of coercion to counteract it
> . . . is consistent.[25]

It is imperative (no pun intended) to note that, for Kant, it is not freedom *per se* that is to be unabridged but, rather, freedom in accord with universal laws. This is, I think, the old notion of 'like liberty for all' which has so recently found eloquent expression in the work of John Rawls.[26]

The exercise of freedom in accordance with universal laws is, of course, nothing other than the principle of autonomy.[27] Thus it is autonomy and not mere spontaneity that is to be preserved. Spontaneity is, of course, a condition of autonomy, but it does not follow from this that spontaneity deserves unbridled protection, even when it is in violation of the law.

Parenthetically, we may note that Kant's view on this point indicates where he would have to stand on the issue of *mens rea* ('guilty mind') and responsibility, a matter of much concern to legal philosophers such as Hart, Kenny, and Mackie.[28]

C.   Reasons for Acting Morally.

The question whether one can make any sense of asking 'Why should I be moral?' is one that has been much debated. It is surely the case that the great moral philosophers in the history of western phi- losophy have felt that there are points beyond which inquiry cannot penetrate in seeking the grounds of morality. Aristotle, Hume, Kant, and Mill all address the issue of 'first principles', and come to effectively the same conclusion: first

principles of morals (or of any other inquiry,
for that matter) cannot be demonstrated in the
same way as secondary or derivative principles.[29]
The upshot of these observations is that, to the
extent that these philosophers deal with the
question 'Why should I be moral?' at all, the
arguments given in answer to the question will
of necessity take a different form from those
given in support of derivative principles. For
example, Mill argues in one fashion in showing
why one ought not to lie, steal, etc., and in
quite another manner when attempting to justify
the principle of utility itself. The former
mode of argument claims to be 'conclusive' while
the latter does not--at least, not quite.[30]

It would be interesting and profitable to
deal extensively with the ways in which each of
the philosophers mentioned above treats the
matter of first principles. Unfortunately, we
must restrict ourselves to an analysis of Kant's
position.

1.   Plato and the Negation of Hypothetical
     Imperatives.

I think it will help to clarify Kant's position on the question 'Why should I be moral?'
if we take a brief look at Plato. In the
Republic, Socrates debates with Thrasymachus over,
not only the nature of justice, but whether there
was any reason why one ought to be just, if a
case could be made for saying that one could
serve one's own interests more effectively by
being unjust. Clearly, the issue of 'Why should
I be just (moral)?' is one of concern to Plato.

The concern evidenced by Plato in the
Republic can be put in Kantian terms this way:
why should we observe categorical restraints upon
our actions? If the position advocated by
Thrasymachus carries the day, then the requirement to act justly becomes an hypothetical requirement that we ought to act justly because
our interests lie on the side of justice. Should
the premise be false, and our interests lie

elsewhere, the imperative to act justly would be negated.

There is, for Kant, a second way in which an hypothetical imperative can be negated, this being that we abandon the desire that is the ground for the imperative, that provides us with the reason for assenting to the imperative.[31] It has been suggested that the best way of understanding hypothetical imperatives is to conceive of them as presenting a choice, between pursuing the means required by the imperative or abandoning the end which requires that means.[32]

To return to the case of Thrasymachus, it seems that Plato recognizes the legitimacy of the question, 'Why should I be just (moral)?' Clearly, there is difference between the question 'Why should I be moral?' and 'How can I be moral?' The latter question has two senses, one which asks for the specific course of action that will fulfill the requirements of morality in some specific instance, and another more general sense, which ask for the metaphysical conditions of the possibility of morality. In the case of Kant, the metaphysical question is bound up with his analysis of the possibility of freedom (here, in the sense of spontaneity). The obligation to obey the moral law, however, is the distinctively normative side of Kant's argument. There is, of course, a potential problem with speaking of a 'distinctively normative' aspect to Kant's argument: Kant himself says that morality follows analytically from the assumption of freedom.[33] We shall turn to this difficulty presently.

It is worth noting that commentators appear to be of several minds as to how Socrates ought to respond to Thrasymachus, who wants to know what reason there is to act justly, if I can in fact better my station in life by doing the opposite. Phillipa Foot argues that it would be highly unlikely that I could so benefit myself, and thus imprudent to pursue a life of injustice.[34]

Thus the tack is that Thrasymachus' argument rests on a false premise, namely that one can ever have any reasonable expectation of getting on better by being unjust. Since the initial argument is based on a false premise, Foot claims, we need not accept the conclusion. The leaders of organized crime, it may be noted, have not read Ms. Foot's article, and thus do not know that their lifestyle rests on a false premise.

Foot's argument, to be serious once again, has a strong Humean flavor to it:

> Having explained the moral *appro-bation* attending merit or virtue, there remains nothing but briefly to consider our interested *obligation* to it, and to inquire whether every man who has any regard to his own happiness and welfare will not best find his account in the practice of every moral duty.[35]

It is, of course, Hume's view that the practice of the virtues *is* in each individual's true interest.[36] Thus he would agree with Foot's claim that we *cannot* reasonably expect to better ourselves by a life of injustice. As I have already noted, however, Hume's position is not really so much at odds with Kant's.

Many of us, I suspect, will have nothing whatever to do with this line of argument. D. Z. Phillips notes a crucial distinction between what we may call 'general' and 'selective' injustice. The former means being unjust all the time, while the latter involves being unjust only when one believes oneself to have a good chance of getting away with it.[37] The former, Phillips says, is at least logically possible, and it is downright likely that a clever person could bring off the latter. It is not enough to give an answer as to why one ought to avoid general injustice--this may be every bit as imprudent as Foot says--without

answering the question with regard to 'selective'
injustice. Foot's analysis yields no answer to
why one ought to avoid being selectively unjust
when one can get away with it. We lack an answer
to the question why we should be moral all of the
time, and not only at those times when we might
get caught in our immorality. I agree with
Phillips--and with Kant--that considerations of
mere self-interest cannot supply an answer to
this question.[38]

2.   Freedom and Autonomy As Reciprocal Concepts.

        To return now to a difficulty mentioned above,
let us ask whether Kant's claim that morality
follows analytically from the assumption of freedom does not visit havoc on the assertion that
Kant's argument has a uniquely normative dimension. I think that it does not, because, as I
have argued, freedom (spontaneity) and autonomy
(self-legislation) are reciprocal concepts, and
neither can be made fully intelligible in abstraction from the other. This being the case, it becomes clear that Kant is not deriving a normative
law from a principle (spontaneity) that is merely
metaphysical. Wolff refers to Kant's 'derivation'
of autonomy from freedom[39]; since these two concepts are reciprocal, it may be misleading to
speak of 'derivation' here at all, as this gives
the mistaken impression that one of the two notions
contains the other, but is broader than the other
in some substantive sense. Kant, after all, says
that a ". . . free will and a will under moral
laws are identical."[40]

        Why, we may wonder, does Kant begin with spon-
taneity rather than with autonomy at this rather
crucial stage in his argument? I believe that
this is because Kant finds freedom to be presupposed in something to which we are intuitively
committed, namely, the notion that we have a concept of ". . . a being as rational and conscious
of his causality with respect to actions, that is,
as endowed with a will;"[41] Aristotle's concept of

deliberation is perhaps the clearest account of this same phenomenon prior to Kant.[42]

3. Reason: Too Strong or Too Weak?

Also relevant to the discussion of Kant's response to the question 'Why should I be moral?' is R. P. Wolff's claim that, ". . . either reason is too weak to overcome sensuous inclination, in which case we cannot hold the agent responsible . . . or reason is strong enough to overcome sensuous inclination, in which case it will . . ."[43] Either way, if Wolff is right, no sense can be made of the binding force of the categorical imperative--its very 'imperativeness' would be dissipated. But, fortunately for Kant, Wolff is not right.

The principal problem in Wolff's analysis lies, I think, in a failure to distinguish between freedom (spontaneity) and autonomy. The two notions overlap, in that all autonomous actions are spontaneous. Not all spontaneous actions are autonomous, however. Some, those in response to inclination, are clearly heteronomous. Spontaneity, then, is the classification into which all actions fall. It is spontaneity and not autonomy that is the found of responsibility. Thus the dichotomy Wolff poses is a false one. Insofar as we are spontaneous--which must be presupposed if we would think of ourselves as independent rational beings endowed with a will--we must take ourselves as responsible for all our actions, whether we pursue inclination or some other motive. The very concept of spontaneity renders the question of whether reason is strong enough or too weak to overcome inclination a non-issue.

We should also note that the issues of responsibility and culpability are quite separable here. We may be responsible for some wrong-doing, in the sense that it is our action that results in the improper consequences, without being either morally or legally blame-worthy. Responsibility is a necessary condition of culpability, but not a

sufficient one. Much of the commentary on Kant's
moral theory has concentrated so heavily on the
questions of act-description and the problems
that pertain thereto that the issue of the grounds
of responsibility and culpability tend to get lost
in the shuffle. They deserve to see the light
of day.

A failure to understand the distinction between spontaneity and autonomy may arise from confusion over Kant's distinction between Wille and
Willkür. This is not, as we have noted, a distinction Kant draws explicitly in the Grundlegung,
and a certain perplexity about the distinction
might be expected from a reading of that text
alone. The distinction comes clear, however, in
the Metaphysics of Morals and in the Religion, and
Kant's position in the Grundlegung is best understood in the light of these additional texts.

4. Wolff on 'Why Should I be Moral?'

I have already addressed some difficulties
I find in Wolff's treatment of Kant's moral theory.
Specifically, I argued that Wolff's analysis of
the Third Antinomy attributes to Kant a much
stronger view of natural necessity than Kant actually holds. But this is not the only point on
which Wolff and I part company. He thinks that
Kant would have problems even if we were able to
accept the Third Antinomy analysis of the possibility of freedom. Wolff writes,

> . . . even if we accept Kant's
> account of the two standpoints,
> there remains the old problem
> 'Why should I be moral?' . . .
> why should I grant the primacy of
> the noumenal over the phenomenal
> and identify with what Kant assumes
> is the higher or better self?[44]

I, of course, think that we might account for Kant's
answer to 'Why should I be moral?' by reference to

the relations between Kant and the tradition of contract theory. Wolff does not consider this kind
of answer possible under the principles of Kant's
system.[45] I believe that Wolff passes off this
possibility too easily, but I will address this in
the next section. Here, I wish to deal with Wolff's
assertion that even if Kant can answer the question
'Why should I be moral?' in some fashion, his moral
theory still fails to provide what is needed:

> . . . he [Kant] would still be
> faced with the greatest difficulty
> of all, namely, that the only moral
> law derivable from the nature of
> reason is a purely formal law of
> self-consistency which serves to
> rule out inconsistent policies but
> does not, and cannot, serve to
> select some specific consistent
> policies rather than others.[46]

What Wolff says is true, of course, but one wonders
why it ought to be counted as a criticism of Kant.
If each of several possible courses of action is
permissible, why should there be a purely rational
way of deciding between them? I see nothing in
Kant's project for his moral theory as he establishes it in the Grundlegung that would suggest
that he intends for his theory to tell us which
of several possible permissible actions we ought
to perform. So far as the moral worth of actions
is concerned, we cannot say of two actions that,
while each is of moral worth, one is more morally
worthy than the other--to do so would be to violate Kant's view that moral value is beyond price.[47]

Wolff says that, since Kant's theory cannot
select from a list of permissible actions that it
fails to achieve its purpose. Wolff writes,

> . . . therefore the Categorical Im-
> perative can never be, as Kant
> wanted it to be, an a priori valid
> substantive test of the rightness

210

of wrongness of every possible
human policy.[48]

If by 'testing the rightness or wrongness' Wolff
means that we can determine that some one particular action is obligatory in every case where we
have to decide how to act, then I simply do not
think that Kant ever tried to do what Wolff is
suggesting here. In speaking of the 'humanity'
formulation of the categorical imperative, Kant
writes, "The principle of humanity and of every
rational creature as an end in itself is the
supreme limiting condition on freedom of the
actions of each man."[49] The phrase 'supreme limiting condition' is crucial here. It suggests
that Kant's goal is to show how we may not act
(morally) with regard to persons. Thus the claim
is that, for any proposed policy, we may discover
whether it is permissible. If it is not, then
we may not act on it. If it is permissible, then
we have a further task, namely that of discovering
whether it is also obligatory, that is, whether
its contrary is prohibited. If a policy is obligatory, then we must do it. All that Kant's theory
alleges to guarantee, so far as I can tell, is that
we can, for any proposed maxim of action, determine
the category into which it falls, permissible, prohibited, or obligatory. This is the only sense in
which Kant would claim to be able to pick among
permissibles on purely rational grounds, nor can I
think of any reason why he should have to.

D.   The Contract Model.

    The last thing to be considered here is also
the most crucial to my analysis of Kant: the contract theory model of obligation. I have already
argued that the concept of an 'ideal contract'
among rational beings is Kant's 'normative vehicle'.
It is time to consider some objections to this
analysis, and some further evidence in support
to it.

211

1.   Objections to the Contract Model.

One noted commentator who finds the notion
of the contract as a key to understanding Kant's
position unpromising is, once again, R. P. Wolff.
I think, needless to say, that Wolff is wrong
about this, though his view about the contract
model is consistent with the other things he says
about Kant.

Wolff writes, ". . . we must ask whether Kant
meant us to imagine the Kingdom of Ends as a community whose members enact binding law through a
process of collective deliberation."[50] It is my
view that this is just what Kant asks us to imagine.
Wolff, however, says,

> The answer is clearly no. The mem-
> bers of the Kingdom of Ends achieve
> unanimity in their moral legisla-
> tion not by collective deliberation,
> but by each one independently legi-
> slating for himself, as though he
> were legislating for all . . .[51]

Wolff further thinks that, since all rational
beings cannot help but legislate the same law,
any notion of communication among them is inci-
dental to their arriving at unanimity.[52] Two
points are relevant here: (1) Wolff seems to
be mistaken about what he evidently sees as a
distinction between Kant and Rousseau on the
nature of the 'original contract'; (2) although
what Wolff says about the role of communication
in arriving at unanimity is true, this is really
irrelevant to the central issue. We want to know
why we are bound, not how we came to be unanimous.

To understand Rousseau's conception of the
'general will', we must note how that will is determined: it is determined by each individual
asking him- or herself what course of action would
be most appropriate for everyone.[53] Thus the image
is precisely that of each legislating for all--
the same image that we find in Kant. There are

significant differences between Kant and Rousseau, particularly regarding Rousseau's utilitarian leanings, which Kant would surely not accept. These dissimilarities have been noted in the preceding chapter. There is not, however, a major dissimilarity between Kant and Rousseau on the important point under discussion here.

It is also important to note that it is not clear that Kant's analysis of universal legislation is as devoid of any notion of 'communication' among rational beings as Wolff suggests it is. Kant writes, "Reason, therefore, relates every maxim of the will as giving universal laws *to every other will* . . ."[54] This sounds like the classic conception of each person contracting with each other person that finds perhaps its clearest expression in Hobbes: ". . . as if every man should say to every other man, *I authorise and give up my Right of Governing my selfe*, . . ."[55]

Finally, and most importantly, the point of the concept of contract is to explain how we can conceive of ourselves as bound by the moral law and not, as Wolff seems to think, to account for the fact that the moral law is the same for each person. I think that the reason Wolff runs afoul of this distinction is that he takes the wrong conception of what such an 'ideal contract' should decide as his starting-point. His criticism of the notion of an 'ideal contract' is essentially that such a contract, even if one were possible, could not produce a set of binding principles. Wolff writes,

> Since the Categorical Imperative is only a necessary condition for the objective validity of principles, it cannot by itself identify a set of substantive principles as universally binding.[56]

This remark is of a piece with Wolff's later criticism that Kant's position, ". . . cannot serve to

213

select some specific consistent policies . . ."[57]
My response here is the same as the one I made
earlier: Wolff's analysis of Kant's position
simply requires too much. It asks, not only more
than Kant can deliver, but more than it is at all
reasonable to require a theory to deliver.

I suggested in the preceding chapter that
Rawls' version of contract theory is the most
illuminating in connecting with Kant. It seems
appropriate to reiterate this point here. The
purpose of Rawls' use of the contract is to
account for our obligation to his two principles
of justice; Kant's purpose is to account for our
obligation to the categorical imperative. The
level of 'substantive principles' of which Wolff
speaks would be reached, for Rawls, at the 'con-
stitutional convention' and not, decidedly, at
the point of the 'original contract'.

There is a second kind of objection to a contract theory analysis of Kant's moral theory, which
ought to be addressed briefly before I move on to
offer further evidence in support of the interpretation. I do not associate this objection with
anyone in particular, but I imagine it arising. It
might be said that contract theory is, after all,
a social doctrine and, as such, it cannot be employed to account for moral obligation, since this
is an individual matter. This objection is just
wrong-headed, on several counts.

First of all, I see no grounds, either historical or philosophical, for making such a sharp
distinction between moral and social theory, between, as it were, ethics and politics. Aristotle
obviously draws no such sharp separation and, as
I have argued, Kant is like Aristotle in many philosophically important ways. It is clear that Kant's
first principle in social philosophy is essentially
the categorical imperative once again.[58]

This last remark leads to a second response.
For Kant, morality is very much a social phenomenon.
It is because of what we share in common with all

214

rational beings (spontaneity and self-legislation)
that morality is possible at all. Morality therefore assumes a certain concept of community.

We are lead to a third objection, one made,
implicitly at least, by G. E. M. Anscombe. She
argues, in effect, that the concept of self-legislation is an absurdity, because the notion of
legislation is itself a public one.[59] I think
Miss Anscombe misunderstands Kant's concept of
legislation.[60] If self-legislation meant that
each individual would do as he or she pleased,
quite apart from any considerations about others,
that would be absurd. As we have seen, however,
this is simply not what Kant means by self-legislation. Hence, the objection fails.

2.   Further Evidence in Support of the Contract
      Model.

There are further arguments to be presented
in support of the contract theory analysis of
Kant's moral philosophy. I suppose that this material might have been presented in the preceding
chapter, but it may be more effective here, juxta-
posed as it is with the objections to the contract theory interpretation. It will be possible
here to clarify further the precise sense of
'contract' I intend.

Alan Donagan presents several illuminating
examples in his recent book, The Theory of Morality.[61]
He describes a group of 'potholers' (a quaint and
perhaps antiquated term for cave explorers) who
find themselves in the following sort of dilemma:
one of their number is stuck in the only path out
of the cave; the only way he can be gotten out
safely is by being dug out slowly; however, the
others will drown from rising water unless the
opening is blasted open with explosives, which
would kill the man trapped in the opening. What
are the 'potholers' to do?[62] Donagan might have
approached the problem from a utilitarian point of
view, and reached the same conclusion he in fact

215

reaches: that it is permissible to blast away.
However, Donagan thinks that utilitarianism has
other problems--even though it may come up with
what he sees as the right answer in this case--
and opts for another sort of solution at the level
of theory. He refers to the sorts of decisions
that persons engaged commonly in what they know
to be a dangerous venture would agree to in advance. He thinks they would commit themselves
(morally) to abiding by certain principles of decision in concrete cases. The binding force on
later decisions seems, on Donagan's view, to arise
from the notion of prior commitment--from contract. All that Donagan's position seems to require in the way of background assumptions in
order for individuals to be thought of as bound
to act in certain ways is that they be aware of
the nature of their activity, of its risks and
possible benefits. This would ensure that no one
would be duped into obligations, by being misled
about the risks involved in 'potholing' or any
other activity.

    What has all of this to do with Kant? There
are several important points of relationship between Donagan's view and the interpretation of
Kant that I have been urging. First, Donagan's
view accounts for our obligation to act or refrain from acting in certain ways by reference to
what it would be reasonable for people to agree to
in advance. That is, that individuals may be
thought of as voluntarily assenting to restrictions
on their private ends. Each of the 'potholers'
would surely have his/her own self-preservation
as a private end, but this would not be the crucial deciding factor. In this regard, Donagan's
view is like that of Rawls, as well as bearing a
resemblance to Kant's position. Rawls argues, it
will be recalled, that we can consider ourselves
bound to certain principles of justice to be used
as 'tools of criticism' in judging the appropriateness of possible or existing social arrangements
because we can imagine ourselves having agreed to
such principles.

Wolff would probably object to this line of
argument by saying that it still does not yield
a set of substantive principles that dictate what
ought to be done in every conceivable case. Indeed not, but, as I have argued, this requirement
is simply too strong. Neither Kant nor Rawls is
seeking a criterion of obligatoriness for every
case; rather, their theories provide criteria of
permissibility. I have already argued for this
point of interpretation of Kant, but let us look
at what Rawls says on the matter:

> These principles are to regulate
> all further agreements; they
> specify the kinds of social coop-
> eration that *can* be entered into
> and the forms of government that
> *can* be established. [63]

It seems clear that Rawls is here presenting criteria of permissibility; prohibition follows from
the observation that a given social arrangement
violates the principles that would be chosen in
the 'original position', while obligatoriness
follows from the observation that any arrangement
other than the given one would violate those principles. Thus, in cases where there is more than
one permissible option, there is no one best way
of proceeding that is obligatory. It might, I
suppose, be objected that Rawls' principles of
justice and Kant's categorical imperative differ
in a significant respect that negates my arguments
relating them. That is, Rawls' view contains a
distribution principle which, it might be argued,
places all possible cases on a gigantic sliding
scale such that any two cases could always be distinguished in terms of the distribution principle.
If this is the case, then Rawls' position would
pick out the best action in each case in a way
in which Kant's categorical imperative does not.
I do not think that Rawls' position in fact has
this consequence. It is quite conceivable, I
should think, that several alternative policies
might have the same distributive consequences.

217

This being the case, there would be no way of
picking among them. But the objection is really
beside the point anyway, insofar as the crucial
point is concerned: both Rawls and Kant view
the concept of contrast as the focal point of a
'tool of criticism' of existing or possible
situations.

E.   Summary.

     I am now ready to sum up my arguments. A
good deal of what has been presented in the course
of this essay has been exegetical in character.
This seemed essential, given the extreme complexity
of Kant's theory, and the fact that important
facets of his views are spread over a range of
writings. There is, though, substantial philosophical content as well, both in terms of trying
to lay out what I take to be the character of
Kant's moral theory, and in terms of arguing for
the viability of that theory.

1.   Kant's Theory of the Will.

     Most of the exegetical work has been directed
towards unpacking Kant's theory of the will, and
to do so in terms of his distinction between Wille
and Willkür. The distinction is, I have argued,
absolutely essential to an understanding of Kant's
moral theory and his theory of rational agency.

     Also crucial to Kant's theory of agency is
his theory of freedom. The very possibility of
freedom is argued for in Kant's analysis of the
Third Antinomy of the first Critique. On this
very significant aspect of Kant's theory, I argue
essentially for two points: (1) that Kant's
theory of the 'causality' of the will and, thus,
his theory of freedom, may best be understood in
terms of the similarities between Kant's views
and Aristotle's doctrine of 'four causes'; (2)
that a substantial amount of the secondary literature on this matter of the Third Antinomy
attributes to Kant a stronger view of natural
necessity than the one he actually holds. I

think the text of the first Critique supports
my analysis.

2.   Kant's Theory of Legislation.

      I have argued that Kant's theory of moral legi-
slation bears strong relations to the tradition of
social contract theory. In particular, I think
that the contemporary theorist John Rawls employs
the notion of the 'original contract' in a way that
is most illuminating for our understanding of Kant,
namely, as a 'tool of criticism'.

      Somewhat in passing, I have also shown how
Kant would have to object to certain utilitarian
theories of legislation. Clarifying the ten-
sions between Kant and the utilitarians would in
itself constitute quite a project, and I would like
someday to sort out where Kant and the utilitarians
agree and where they differ--but not today.

      I have attempted to defend the contract theory
model of Kant's moral philosophy against known objections and also against what seem to me to be
potential objections. I may by now have become so
attached to thinking of Kant in terms of the contract theory analysis that I can no longer appreciate legitimate difficulties with this analysis.
I have nonetheless tried to recognize objections
and to deal with them. Thus I leave the reader
to reach a judgment.

NOTES - Chapter Four

[1]FMM, pp. 406-09.

[2]Ibid., p. 413.

[3]Ibid., p. 417.

[4]Ibid., p. 419.

[5]Cf., Ibid., pp. 412-13; also Lewis White Beck, A Commentary on Kant's Critique of Practical Reason, p. 41.

[6]FMM, pp. 446-47.

[7]Ibid., p. 440.

[8]Virtue, p. 417.

[9]The German term for 'legislation' is, once again, Gesetzgebung.

[10]FMM, p. 440.

[11]Jeffrie Murphy, Kant: The Philosophy of Right, p. 82.

[12]Ibid., p. 83.

[13]FMM, p. 440.

[14]FMM, p. 435.

[15]FMM, p. 434, my emphasis.

[16]This seems to be what Kant proposes in Justice, p. 227.

[17]Justice, p. 227.

[18]FMM, p. 431.

[19]Cf., Ibid., p. 428. Of 'persons', Kant writes,

". . . rational beings are designated 'persons' because their nature indicates that they are ends in themselves."

[20]FMM, p. 440.

[21]Cf., Ibid., p. 426. The moral law, ". . . must be connected (wholly a priori) with the concept of the will of a rational being as such."

[22]This need not mean that there is one and only one 'right action' in any given instance.

[23]Cf., FMM, pp. 441-45.

[24]Cf., Jeffrie Murphy, Op.cit., p. 88.

[25]Justice, p. 231, my emphasis.

[26]Cf., John Rawls, Op.cit., p. 60.

[27]Cf., FMM, pp. 440, 447.

[28]Cf., H. L. A. Hart, Punishment and Responsibility; A. J. P. Kenny, "Intention and Mens Rea in Murder", in Law, Morality, and Society (Oxford, 1977); J. L. Mackie, "The Grounds of Responsibility", Ibid.

[29]Cf., Aristotle, Nicomachean Ethics; Hume, Inquiry, p. 111; FMM, p. 448; Mill, Utilitarianism, Chap. I.

[30]Just what Mill's argument for the principle of utility is, and whether it succeeds in making its point, are matters which have provoked a spate of commentary (Cf., Kai Nielsen, "Mill's Proof of Utility", Bucknell Review, Spring, 1977; G. E. Moore, Principia Ethica. These two sources represent diametrically opposed views of the nature and status of Mill's 'proof'--there are many other commentaries on both sides of the question.)

[31]For an interesting recent discussion of desires and reasons see Thomas Nagel, The Possibility

221

of Altruism (Oxford, 1970).

[32]Cf., Alan Donagan, The Theory of Morality (Chicago, 1977).

[33]FMM, pp. 447, 449, 462.

[34]Cf., P. Foot, "Moral Beliefs," reprinted in Ethics, edited by Thomson and Dworkin, pp. 239-60. (Henceforth, this anthology will be referred to as 'Thomson and Dworkin').

[35]Hume, Inquiry, p. 99.

[36]Ibid., p. 100.

[37]D. Z. Phillips, "Does it Pay to be Good?", in Thomson and Dworkin, pp. 261-78.

[38]This will no doubt be seen as making far shorter shrift of utilitarianism than is warranted by the complexities of that tradition; indeed, it does, and I can only apologize by saying that there's not time to consider everything here.

[39]Wolff refers to Kant's 'derivation' of autonomy from freedom (Cf., Wolff, Op.cit., p. 197); since these two concepts are reciprocal, it may be misleading to speak of 'derivation' here, as this gives the impression that one of the two concepts completely contains the other while being at the same time broader than the other.

[40]FMM, p. 447.

[41]Ibid., p. 449.

[42]Cf., Aristotle, Nicomachean Ethics; also, Richard Taylor, Metaphysics, for a contemporary analysis of the concept of 'deliberation'.

[43]Wolff, Op.cit., p. 211.

[44]Ibid.

[45] _Ibid._, pp. 181-86.

[46] _Ibid._, p. 211.

[47] Cf., _FMM_, p. 435.

[48] Wolff, _Op.cit._, p. 212.

[49] _FMM_, pp. 439-41, my emphasis.

[50] Wolff, _Op.cit._, p. 183.

[51] _Ibid._

[52] _Ibid._

[53] Cf., Rousseau, _The Social Contract_.

[54] _FMM_, p. 434, my emphasis.

[55] Hobbes, _Leviathan_, p. 227.

[56] Wolff, _Op.cit._, p. 185.

[57] _Ibid._, p. 211.

[58] Cf., _Justice_, pp. 230-31.

[59] Cf., G. E. M. Anscombe, "Modern Moral Philosophy," in _Thomson and Dworkin_, pp. 186-210.

[60] Parenthetically, Wolff also misunderstands Kant's concept of legislation. In _In Defense of Anarchism_, Wolff claims that Kant's position commits him to a 'philosophical anarchism'. I think Wolff says this because he confuses spontaneity and autonomy. Something of the same confusion seems implicit in Anscombe.

[61] Alan Donagan, _Op.cit._

[62] _Ibid._, pp. 177-80.

[63] John Rawls, _Op.cit._, p. 11, my emphasis.

INDEX

Act description, 42-48.

Anscombe, G. E. M., 215.

Appearances and things-in-themselves, 68-75.

Aristotle, 25-26, 28-33, 35, 37-38, 65-67, 75, 81, 87, 94-95, 138, 140, 207-208, 214, 218.

Beck, L. W., 35-36, 52-53, 75-77, 99fn, 106-107, 122.

Bentham, J., 100-101fn, 123-126, 128-130, 172.

Choice, 24, 26-43; and deliberation, 28-30; and Willkür, 81.

Constraint (Nötigung), 21-24, 31, 105, 194.

Contract theory, 103, 108, 148-178, 181, 211-217, 219.

Donagan, A., 215-216.

Duty, 115-116, 119, 121-122, 133-135; perfect v. imperfect, 136-137, 143-144, 186fn.

Foot, P., 205-207.

Four causes, 65-67, 81-89, 94, 218.

Freedom and autonomy, 26, 197, 203; and legislation, 104, 123, 144-147, 180-181; negative freedom, 197; freedom and obligation, 105, 145-147, 168, 182fn.; positive freedom, 197; freedom and spontaneity, 81-82; 106, 109, 197, 202-203.

Happiness, 138.

Hare, R. M., 40, 82.

Hobbes, T., 155-161, 171, 175, 178.

Hume, D., 13-16, 126-128, 130-131, 206.

Imperatives, categorical, 20, 47, 52, 144-145, 168, 180-181, 194-195, 201, 214; imperatives, hypothetical, 108-110, 205.

Ladd, J., 151.

Legislation and autonomy, 23, 103-107, 111, 115, 135-136, 145-147, 152-154, 178-180, 191fn., 195, 202; ethical v. juridical, 113-114, 120; internal v. external, 112-123, 157; moral, 111-123; and obligation, 103, 132-136, 145-147, 152-154; by *Wille*, 12, 87-89, 96, 112.

Leibniz, G., 26-28.

Marx, K., 143-144.

Maxim, 40-43, 93-95, 211; and motives, 41-43, 49-51.

Mill, J. S., 129-132, 198, 221fn.

Moral epistemology, 48-55; and maxims, 48-51, 54.

Moral worth, 22, 39, 91-95, 114.

Moore, G. E., 81-82, 103, 168.

Murphy, J., 99fn., 198-200, 202.

Necessity, 16-19, 68, 77-80, 218; and necessitation, 59fn.

Nell, O., 43, 47-48, 55.

Obligation, 103, 133-136, 145-147, 151, 153, 178-180, 183fn., 185fn., 193-194, 205, 214.

Phillips, D., 206.

Plato, 204-205.

Practical reason, 12-16, 106-107, 195.

Rawls, J., 165-177, 216-217.

Realm of ends and obligation, 37, 152-154, 158-161, 175-178; and sovereignty, 152-154, 162, 175.

Ross, D., 87-88, 94-95.

Rousseau, J-J., 148-151, 161-165, 187-188fn., 212.

Sartre, J-P., 37.

Silber, J., 75, 86-87.

Singer, M., 43-47.

Smart, J., 164.

Third antinomy, 67-80, 218.

'Two standpoints' doctrine, 181.

Utilitarianism, 123-132, 163-165, 213, 222fn.

Will, autonomy of, 81-82, 87, 110, 150-151, 179-180, 188fn., 191fn., 196, 199, 207-208; causality of, 65-67, 80-97, 108; determination of, 16-19, 111; heteronomy of, 87; holy will, 19-26, 33-34, 59-60fn., 84, 122, 133; spontaneity of, 67, 81-82, 109-110, 116-117, 147, 207-208; as Wille, 7-13, 26, 65, 83-89, 95-96, 196-199; Wille/Willkür distinction, 7-13, 26, 103-106, 160, 179-180, 193, 196-197, 199, 218; as Willkür, 7-13, 24-26, 34, 55-57, 65, 67-75, 80-82, 88, 105-107, 110, 196-199.

Wolff, R., 74-75, 115, 138-142, 148-149, 207-214, 217, 222-223fn.